The First Editorial

By JOAN LEESE

Newsletter 1, 1971

In the first issue in 1971 of the Newsletter, later to be called the Journal, Joan Leese the editor wrote:

'One of our purposes in this Newsletter is to keep members in touch with information as it comes to light, from outsiders as in the letters below, and from our meetings, field days and our own discoveries. All members can contribute in the last-named way by sending in anything which they are told or which they perceive for themselves - anything, however meagre, however absurd, may have a grain of truth in it or lead to a grain of truth, and here it can be recorded so that it will be available for future use.

Our other purpose is to report local history as it is happening. Our landscape is being changed by house building, road alterations and new agricultural methods. Let us know about such activities in your parish. And, equally important, about your parochial life, which is affected by these activities and affects them.

Recently I read some words which appealed very much to me, and I hope you will appreciate them too. They come from *The Historian's Craft* by the distinguished French historian, Marc Bloch: "Behind the features of the landscape, behind tools or machinery, behind what appears to be the most formalized written documents, and behind institutions, which seem almost entirely detached from their founders, there are men, and it is men that history seeks to grasp. Failing that, it will be at best but an exercise in erudition. The good historian is like the giant of the fairy tale. He knows that wherever he catches the scent of human flesh, there his quarry lies."'

Tower House

Newsletter 1, 1971

Among the many reactions to our book, *Bromyard: A Local History,* are letters from Dr. W. W. Wells, who practised here for sixteen years and now in his ninetieth year lives at Whitchurch, Cardiff, and his son Dr. John Wells, who married the daughter of the late Mr. W. T. Barneby of Saltmarshe Castle. Both correspondents question our use of the name, Tower House, for their old home, Dr. Wells saying, 'We called it Tower Hill House and as such it appeared in the telephone directory, etc. First Miss Woodhouse and later Mr. Foster, a bank manager, lived above us in Tower House.'

Dr. Wells gives the following interesting account of his restorations of the house:

'I came to Bromyard in 1920 and bought what I understood as Tower Hill House from Father Denys Mathieu, O.S.B., for a very small sum. When I bought the house it was covered with a layer of stucco of a greyish colour, up to the level where the ornamental woodwork lies beneath the eaves. The N.E. side contained one sash window, one on each floor: the N. side the same. There were four large rooms all looking onto the street. The one on the left hand side of the front door upstairs, was a very handsome room panelled to the ceiling with old oak square panels, made with an adze, and a magnificent oak floor of very wide and thick boards. The original fireplace had been replaced by a much later one. The other upstairs room was also panelled, but with very large panels at a much later date. The left-hand downstairs room, with an enormous door, was plastered and has a large plaster ornament on the ceiling, and a very fine Adam type mantelpiece. The other room had the original open fire, filled in with an erection of the very handsome bedpost. This we afterwards removed and revealed the open fireplace. The room was not plastered on the road side, but the outside woodwork was visible.

During one winter, the stucco came off from under the window of the panelled room and revealed two beams; on the strength of this, I took the risk and employed a local bricklayer, Thomas Handley, to strip the whole house and found it was a black and white house, made of large and smaller beams with plastered oak laths between them, covered with a heavy plaster outside and in containing a large amount of hair. Mr. Handley renovated many of the larger beams which had rotted under the stucco, with concrete and Mr. Barneby very kindly gave us some oak for the smaller one; the whole was then creosoted and painted like it looks now. When the stucco was removed from around the two sash windows to the left of the front-door the shape of the original windows was located by the position of the beams. The windows on the right-hand side had apparently never been altered. I presume the four sash windows were put in late in the eighteenth or early in the nineteenth century.

Father Denys could tell me nothing about the history of the house, but that when he cleaned it, he had found evidence that it had been used to store grain. With reference to the tradition that Charles I slept there I was told that he was the guest of Mrs. Baynham but slept at the Bishop's Palace. As soon as the work of changing the

BROMYARD

ROUND AND ABOUT

edited

by

Deborah Waller

THE BROMYARD AND DISTRICT LOCAL HISTORY SOCIETY
BROMYARD
HEREFORDSHIRE
1991

Published by

The Bromyard and District Local History Society

©

ISBN 0 9502068 5 7

[1] Out of print
[2] Shortly to be re-issued

Printed by
Orphans Press Ltd.,
Leominster, Herefordshire
HR6 8JT

CONTENTS

MAPS

ACKNOWLEDGEMENTS

The Publication Committee of the Bromyard and District Local History Society would like to thank all contributors to the Newsletters and Journals over the years, especially those whose articles appear in this publication. We are also very grateful to all the people who have let the Society make copies of their photographs from which those in the book have been drawn, including the University of Cambridge Committee for Aerial Photography, the Woolhope Naturalists' Field Club, and Castle Frome Parochial Church Council. The oil painting of the Market Hall on the front cover, artist unknown, and the watercolour of Avenbury Church have been reproduced with the kind permission of local owners.

We would also like to thank Harold Rhodes who designed the front and back covers, Peter Russell and Barry Stephenson for preparing the maps, and Charles Grant for his drawings. Rita Hassell gave us the booklet 'Pearl above Rubies'.

Once more, a warm appreciation to Tony Hicks and his staff of Orphans' Press.

Preface

My dictionary defines an Anthology as 'A choice collection of passages from literature ...', and 'Bromyard Round and About' offers the reader just such a collection. The Bromyard and District Local History Society has had a newsletter or journal for twenty years and it was thought that many of the original articles would be of interest to a wider public. Also included are newspaper stories and other material drawn from the collections of papers amassed by the Society in the twenty-five years since its inception. These articles, which follow a figure-of-eight route through Bromyard and the parishes roundabout, are seen as the first of a series which it is hoped will be published from time to time. They are not in chronological order and many things have changed since they were written.

The tour starts with a doctor in Bromyard and some other items in the town, before going to The Downs and Norton and then along the lane to Avenbury, Jumper's Hole, Castle Frome and Cheyney Court, and back via Burley Gate, Stoke Lacy and Pencombe to Bromyard, where the 'Bromyard Fire Service' safeguards both town and country. Out again on the figure-of-eight to Winslow and Grendon Bishop and far-flung Wolferlow. Hence to Tedstone Delamere and back on 'Rural Rides' to Bromyard finishing with another doctor in the town.

DEBORAH WALLER, 1991

2

The Bromyard Vicarage Fête used to be one of the social events of the year. This photograph, taken some time in the 1950s, shows the balloon race stall.

Tower House before and after Dr. Wells's restoration in 1920s.

outside of the house was finished I had a letter from the Board of Works in London asking me if I was willing to have the house registered as a house of historic interest, which I agreed to, so I presume it is still and the panels may not be removed.

The original staircase had been removed. The house as it now is was altered to make it appear as it was in 1630 except there was only one gable window to the attic then.'

The Bromyard Bushel

Of the Bromyard Bushel Dr. Wells says: '... it was in the possession of Miss Davies of Broad Street, and she gave it to me as I was living in Mr. Baynham's house. I have a snapshot of both the big rooms, in the parlour is the bushel beside the Adam fireplace as a log basket and the panelling can be seen in the other. I gave it to the church when I left in June 1936.'

Dr. Wells mentions that Miss Davies gave the Bushel to his father, and continues: 'Miss Davies was the sister of Mr. Davies of Davies & Owen, grocers, whose shop was then on the corner of Frog Lane. Mr. Owen moved after Mr. Davies's death to a shop near the Square, between I think the jeweller and Mrs. Passey, a baker. My father had his surgery in 26 (Broad Street), after Miss Davies moved up the New Road. I cannot tell you how the bushel came to Miss Davies.'

But another correspondent, Miss Joan Hatton, of Hereford, does have some information on the matter. She writes:

'My old friend, Miss Miriam Davies, was the daughter of Mr. James Davies who owned a successful grocery and provision business in Broad Street, No. 10 then at the top of Frog Lane. His warehouse and private garden extended down the lane as far as the tanyard premises. The Bromyard Bushel was discovered in the garden acting as a water butt. It was rescued and carefully preserved in the house. It was thought to have come from Tower Hill probably because of the name of Baynham inscribed upon the rim. Mr. J. Davies and his wife were members of the Society of Friends and must have attended Meetings at the old Meeting House of which I knew nothing.'

How fascinating is the problem of how the Bushel got into the garden in Frog Lane! The shop mentioned by Dr. Wells to which Mr. Owen moved is 44 Broad Street now occupied by Mr. Arrowsmith.

[Bromyard Bushel Measure can be seen in Bromyard Church and is inscribed: 'The Bromyard Bushell by Act of Parliament 1670 Herbert (Croft) Lord Bishop of Hereford, John Baynham Gent.' The bishop of Hereford was the lord of the manor of Bromyard and John Baynham who could have lived at Tower House was perhaps his bailiff.

A bushel was used to measure dry goods such as corn, fruit, hops and coal by volume rather than by weight. The Act of 1670 stipulated that wherever corn was sold a standard bushel of eight gallons was to be used and all traders were to submit their own measures to be checked against the official town one. The Bromyard Bushel, cast in bell metal by John Martin a bell founder of Worcester, was probably chained to one of the posts of the old Market House. Before it was demolished in 1844, the Market House stood in the Square in front of the Hop Pole (see front cover) - Ed.]

Angel House, Cruxwell Street

By J. G. SANDERS

Newsletter 3, 1972

Angel House, which was demolished in 1957 and whose site is now part of the car park, was where my family lived for many years. [History rolls on, the Angel House site is now under the new Leisure Centre - Ed. 1991.] My father had a tailor's shop there in 1900, and it was where I was born in 1902, and also my three brothers, the older one in 1899 and the two younger ones in 1905 and 1906.

There were our neighbours whom I remember, a Mrs. Maddy and her daughter, in 1902. But according to *Kelly's Directory* a Mr. Wilkes lived in that house in 1900. He was Collector to the Guardians and also the Relieving Officer for No. 1 district of Bromyard. Then he moved his home and office to a private house in Church Street. He was also the School Attendance Officer for the Rural District. I do not remember him at Angel House, of course, but I very well remember him when he was living in Church Street.

Angel House was heavily timbered similar to the Falcon and Tower House; inside were many old oak timbers and an old oak staircase. There were three rooms downstairs, one of which was my father's shop and the only one visible from Cruxwell Street or 'Top of the Town' as it was very often called. The house had three bedrooms and an attic, also two flights of stairs.

'Top of the Town' with Angel Place.

Mrs. Maddy's house was also of old oak timber, but much larger than ours because it had two bedrooms over the archway which led to the blacksmith's house, shop and pentice, and garden plots for each house at the back, but the blacksmith's premises were not part of Angel House. I very well remember that Mrs. Maddy used to take in boarders occasionally and at General Election times to let off one or two rooms as committee rooms. In those days much excitement was caused by the different parties, but there were only two then, Tory and Liberal. I well remember a verse which was very well sung when the Tory candidate was Rankin and the Liberal one Lamb; it was as follows:-

'Vote, vote for Jimmy Rankin,
   He's the man to do us good.
But if it is Lamb and his wife
   We'll scare 'em with a knife
Then they won't come voting any more.'

In front of each house was a small flower bed and lawn with railings round them, and in front of Mrs. Maddy's house was a well with a stone trough and pump of which I have photographs. Possibly the street name of Cruxwell may have originated from this well for I do not think there was another one in the street. There was a council mains water pump in Cruxwell Street opposite to the White Horse Inn, also two other similar pumps, one in the Old Road and one in Pump Street, but they looked like pump heads, having mains water with a tap.

I am sure that if the plaster which covered the whole of Angel House had been removed there would have been discovered a very fine ancient building similar to the Falcon and Tower House, and also to the timbered black and white house in Sheep Street near the new Catholic Church where my mother was born. Her maiden name was Corbett and that was where her family lived.

I have many recollections of Bromyard. How we spent our leisure and schooldays, and many times paid a visit each year to Powells, the Progress Stores, in Broad Street [now Sunderlands - Ed.] to see the effigy of Father Christmas in the window, and what a thrill it gave us children in those days.

Mr. J. G. Sanders died in October 1974 to the sorrow of all members who knew him and had consulted him on Bromyard life in the first years of this century. A master baker living and working in Hereford it was obvious that his heart was still very much in Bromyard, and he joined the Society soon after its foundation. His friendly kindly manner and willingness to help with information were greatly appreciated.

He has left a lasting memorial and a priceless comprehensive record in the John Sanders Collection of photographs which he generously presented to the Society at the 1973 annual general meeting. We remember him with gratitude and affection.

Newsletter 7, 1974

Annie Roberts - Her Letter

Journal 12, 1989

Miss Annie Roberts lived for many years in a cottage on the top of Hardwick Banks in Winslow, and her memories were useful to the newly fledged History Society. As many new members will never have heard of Miss Roberts, her letter is published here as it is full of interest.

Hardwick Bank,
Bromyard

begun on - Jan 29, 1969.

'Dear Williams,

First, the cattle were sold in the New Road just above the Rose & Lion Inn - not to my knowledge in High Street. The market was held every fortnight, and the men who brought the animals stayed to look after them. They had a hurdle between each cow. The new market hall (built 1843) opposite the post office was never used much,

The new market hall on the right.

it was not central enough and people would not buy anything there if they could help it. The poultry was sold on the pavement at the Falcon Inn - their feet tied together so that they could not get away.

The Tin church I don't remember. The Baptist Church. No. We came to Bromyard in the end of 1879 and there was no Baptist Church there then - My father was a Baptist and went to the Wesleyan Church as the nearest thing.

It may be of interest to know that every first of May was a Hiring Mop, and the folk who wanted servants male or females came to the High Street to look for them. A house maid wore a cap and apron, cooks carried a spoon and fork. Waggoners wore a band of hay in their hats.

The house which is now the Book Shop [Now 5 Broad Street - Ed.] was owned by a man named Tarbeth who kept a livery stable. There was no transport to the outlying villages, he used to take his brake to meet the train in case anyone needed his help.

Now the church here had to supply Grendon Bishop and the Rev Martin had to employ him (Tarbeth) to take him there every Sunday and so they were good friends. This is a bit of fun. One day Rev Martin was going to the station to meet his daughter and Mr Tarbeth overtook him and said 'Oh good morning Bishop of Bromyard' to which Rev Martin said 'Oh good morning publican and sinner you are'. You see Mr Tarbeth kept a public house. The place which is now the Church Institute, Kirkham Garden, was built by Mr. Phipps of Buckenhill for the use of the navvies working on the railway, making from Bromyard to Steens Bridge, as a place for them after work, where they could stay and enjoy themselves instead of the public houses.

The other transport in these days was the carriers cart which held about 6 to 8 people, which went to Hereford on Wednesday and Leominster on Friday. Oh dear I hope I shall not get a swelled head with so much thinking.

It may interest you to know that the road to Hereford came up the Old Road, along Panniers Lane and on to Hereford. The road to Leominster came up the Old Road, turned in at the fork of Stallards Bank, up three fields - which is now all built on - passed the Stone House and along the field next to the Stone House and out on the Leominster road just by Keephill.

Did you know that in these days there was no water, but the wells which had pumps. There was one in Sheep Street, one in Pump Street, one in Schallenge Walk, one by The Crown & Sceptre, one in the Tan House Yard. There is or was one in the passage of Nunwell House, hence its name. I could show you just where it is for my father put a covering over it when the front of Nunwell House was added.

Food was cheaper and far more good than it is now. Bread was 4½d. for a 4 pound loaf and if anyone bought a dozen they had 13. Sugar was 2 pound for 4d. Ham 10d. per pound. Bacon best cuts 8d. There was in those days 6 Bakers' Shops here, Lewis, Payne, Vaughan, Partridge, Taylor, Mitchell, and it was bread then not a mixture of goodness knows what. Oh dear I am giving my age away, it just shows how plain food gave you strength.

I have just thought you could buy fresh herring 24 for a shilling and boned and filleted they were a treat. Eggs at 24 for a shilling.

I think I have answered all your questions if not write again and ask more. You can omit anything you wish but I write as I think of it - bit by bit.

Yours sincerely   Annie Roberts.'

[The Church Institute was taken down in 1989 - Ed.]

A Tourist's Impression of Bromyard

BROMYARD FARMERS AND INTEMPERANCE

The following paragraph appeared in Saturday's *Daily Telegraph,* under the heading "In Wales with a motor, by a tourist":-

"It was at Bromyard, a small market town on the way to Worcester, that we had an experience one is more apt to read about than meet with. It was market day, the pavements were strewed with live and dead chickens, rabbits, boxes of eggs, and other dairy produce. At the inn we were ushered into a regular farmers' ordinary. Some eight or nine farmers were at lunch. At one end of the table stood a huge sirloin of beef cut saddle-wise; at the other end was an equally admirable haunch of lamb. Our host of the rubicund countenance presided with fork and carver, giving a pleasant salutation to the stranger, joining in the flow of talk, and ready to fill up any plate that required replenishing. So we had a cut of most tender beef, good vegetables, plum pie, custard, jam tart, Stilton cheese, and a glass of ale for two shillings; all excellent. The next day, much nearer home, we had more beef of fair quality, vegetables not quite cooked, a pie with crust that would neither bend nor break, a great display of napery, the ceaseless attention of innumerable flies, and no beer, for three shillings, and the hotel was twice as ornate as the little inn. These jovial-looking farmers were discussing the Licensing Bill. One, evidently the wag of the party, argued that it was ridiculous to make the publican pay for a license. 'What you want to do,' he declared, 'Is to make everyone who wants to drink take out a license, same as a dog, only five bob a year. Then if he gets drunk suspend his license for three months, and if he cannot show his license he won't get his drink.' Really if he went into the suggestion Mr Lloyd-George might find it a way to pay for his old age pensions."

Bromyard News & Record, 17.9.1908

Public Entertainments 1883-1901

By JOAN LEESE

Journal 1, 1978

As we know very well, having been told often enough, our forbears had to make their own entertainment, so what did they devise for their amusement during the long Victorian winter evenings and the few public holidays?

The calendars of the *Bromyard News,* 1883-1894, and the copies of the *Bromyard Record,* 1897-1901, give plenty of information on the subject for this district. They mention concerts, balls, dances among the diversions as well as sporting activities, and also visits from professional theatrical companies which show that our forbears did not continually entertain themselves.

Throughout the 1880s there was an annual summer flower show with sports, and Bromyard Races were held each year. A Cherry Feast on the Downs, near the Union, in July 1886 sounds idyllic. Occasion for extra junketing was provided by the Queen's Diamond Jubilee in June 1887 when an ox was roasted and the children walked in procession to the Downs for sports and amusements.

An agricultural depression and a severe winter must have had a lowering effect on local spirits during 1886-87, and the depression, affecting trade as well, continued during 1888, which perhaps accounts for numbers being down at Bromyard Races in May. Let us hope the visit of Fosset's Monster Circus and Hippodrome in June cheered people up. As one of the definitions of the word, 'hippodrome', is a course for chariot races, presumably local blood was stirred, and perhaps local nerves frayed, by scenes more characteristic of the worst excesses of the Roman Empire than suitable for the recreation of the British one at its zenith, but what of that if it raised the spirits of the onlookers. In September the Cambrian Theatre was in the town, under the patronage of Lord St. John, with an entire change of programme every evening.

Throughout the 1880s an unfortunate form of entertainment, drunkenness, was common, and to combat it a social club and reading room for working men was opened in November 1889.

Bromyard Races and the horticultural shows continued annually through the 1890s. There was a men's hockey team, and cricket and football were played in their seasons.

An item in September 1893 tells us that the proprietors of the Star Theatre were granted a month's extension to their licence so presumably they were having a successful time. Unfortunately in November their building or tent was blown to the ground and literally smashed up, providing extra drama for the locals, but the company moved into the Temperance Hall and continued to give performances. The following month the Hall was the scene of more drama, a production by the Bromyard Amateur Dramatic Society.

In the summer of 1897 the *Bromyard Record* was founded from which the rest of my information comes.

Bromyard Orchestra at Little Bridge House c1910.

A flourishing musical society gave concerts during the last years of the century, and in January 1898 held a conversazione. The first quarter of this particular year was full of social activity. In January alone, apart from the conversazione, the Rovers F.C. held a dinner and then a dance, the Wesleyans had a social tea and concert, and then what the *Record* described as 'the most enjoyable function of the season', was an invitation ball at the Hop Pole Hotel. There was professional entertainment from Herr Pareezer's Dioramas and Prussian Choir which offered according to their advertisement, 'Dioramic effects, Charming Tableaux'. The hockey club held an invitation ball, the musical society presented a cantata, and the Rovers F.C. staged a mid-Lent carnival.

But apparently many people did indeed prefer to stay at home making their own entertainment for the Local Odds and Ends section of the *Record* carried the following item on 14th April, the opening words of which show that careless sub-editing is not a modern affliction of newspapers:-

'It seems like as if Bromyard people had given up the idea of attending any more public entertainments in the town, for on the Lady Mascotte variety company visiting Bromyard 2 nights last week, they did not play on the Thursday night because there were only 15 people present, while on the Saturday night some 30 were only present - the manager taking the magnificent sum of 11/8 in the 2 nights. The show of its class - a music hall one - was very good and it seems a pity when companies do come here that they do not meet with better support. Still, Bromyard people complain about the place being dull.

It is hoped the Rovers Minstrel Entertainment which takes place next Tuesday at the Public Hall, will not meet with such a cool reception.'

The following week the paper reported that the Rovers' production had been 'a great success, both from an entertainment point of view and financially', which was not surprising as they probably had more local friends than the unfortunate Lady Mascotte variety company.

The issue of 14th April also reported drama of a different kind, headlined THE GLORIES OF GOOD FRIDAY FOOTBALL with a sub-heading of 'A Broken Leg and A Fractured Jaw Bone'. The sports correspondent pointed out that in the opinion of many readers the games ought not to have taken place on such a day. He continued, 'Bishops Frome, I believe, during the last five years have added two broken legs and a dislocated shoulder to the Good Friday football casualties, so it was with no great surprise I heard last week that the Froomites could not let Good Friday pass without keeping up the record. This they did very effectively and broke a leg'. The casualty was one, Charles Bosley, a rabbit catcher, who was treated in the Cottage Hospital. But Bromyard was not above reproach for the report goes on to say that the fractured jaw was suffered in 'a desperate six-a-side contest for silver medals, between the powerful Sherford-street Swifts and the terrible Sheep-street Runners ... one of the Swifts, Harvey Watkins, (15), ... was pushed by his opponents and in falling one of his own side thoughtfully (?) kicked him in the mouth...', accidentally, one hopes.

The next month Bromyard Steeplechases were held at Drythistle with an attendance larger than the previous year's, 'and it is computed nearly 4,000 arrived by excursions from Birmingham, Wolverhampton, Worcester and Hereford'. Later in May the golf club opened their season, and there were reports of cricket matches throughout the summer.

As there were regular advertisements for bicycles during these last years of the century, probably they were in demand and used for relaxation as well as getting to work and for shopping.

Early in 1899 the Musical Society gave a concert, and an Agricultural and Commercial Invitation Ball was held at the Falcon. Those who preferred out-of-doors entertainment found it at an event reported in the *Record's* issue of 16th February, a mixed hockey match. This was between a local team, the Grasshoppers, and one from Ludlow, whose ladies looked very smart in red skirts, white blouses with broad red ties, white sailor hats with red bands, and tan boots and gloves; they infused an immense amount of enthusiasm into the game. Unfortunately the paper did not think the Bromyard women looked at all smart, but it was a good bustling game which ended in a draw, 1 all. Both the goalkeepers were women.

These diversions were not enough for the *Record* who in an April issue under Local Odds and Ends stated, 'Bromyard has been dull for months, that is to say from an entertainment point of view, but when a company comes here, good, bad, or indifferent, they seem to meet with the same fate - empty houses. Why is it?' The writer goes on to point out that Mr Tom Barger and his talented family were visiting the town the following week, and hoped their performances would be well supported. Elsewhere in the paper is the following advertisement for this company:-

PUBLIC HALL, BROMYARD
For Two nights only TUESDAY AND WEDNESDAY,
May 2nd & 3rd, 1899

ADMISSION - Front Seats (Reserved and numbered) 2s; Second Seats, 1s; a limited number of back seats, 6d. Children under 12 years of age Half-price to first and second seats only. No half-price to back seats. (Special terms for Private Schools). Children in arms not admitted. Doors open at 7.30, overture at 8 sharp, interval at 9, carriages at 10.10, tickets and plan of Hall at the Post Office where seats may be secured in advance.

MR TOM BARGER

assisted by his TALENTED FAMILY in their mirth-provoking and refined ENTERTAINMENT entitled

SOCIETY AND VARIETY

MRS TOM BARGER (Mezzo Soprano and Solo Pianiste). MISS BETA BARGER (Burlesque Actress, Vocalist, Skipping Rope and Skirt Dancer). NORMAN BARGER (Eccentric Vocal Comedian, Grotesque Dancer, High Kicker and inimitable legmania artiste). Young TOM BARGER the droll, quaint little Vocal Comedian. Young T.B. has been christened by the Press a born comedian, a chip off the old block, and a future Dan Leno. The Performance will conclude each evening with a laughable sketch.

Let us hope the Carriage Trade of the town and district appreciated the Bargers as the Bargers appreciated them.

A series of fortnightly dances, with a band in attendance, began at the Royal Oak in May, and in June there was a Sale of Work at Buckenhill when the gramophone kindly lent by Mr Robbins of the Hop Pole, was to be heard. Also in June Bromyard cricketers beat Ludlow, Ludlow scoring 55 and Bromyard 152 for 4, thanks to C. H. Ware who made a century. Even so the *Record* was carping again a few weeks later because the only August Bank holiday attraction was the Wake and Sports on the Downs. With winter a series of smoking concerts began in November at the Hop Pole.

On 14th December the *Record,* pleasure-mad journal, commented, 'It's no good looking on the blue side of everything but Xmas in Bromyard from a social point of view up to now will be very dull. No entertainments or concerts are announced and the only thing on the board is a dance which will take place, we hear, in the Public Hall, on Boxing night.' Was the paper lamenting the lack of advertising, or that of local initiative in amusement making? Although was it a time for junketing with a war on in South Africa?

The following year, 1900, there were the races and the flower show as usual, and in their season football, hockey, cricket and golf. The war itself provided extra entertainment when Bromyard celebrated the relief of Mafeking in May with bell-ringing and fireworks, and a few days later Pretoria Day with a pageant among other activities. In the following January Queen Victoria died which put an end to public entertainment for a while.

Looking back over this period it seems that the district then was very like it is now with entertainment enough for those prepared to go to it, despite the Record's periodic carpings.

Norton Downs Sports and Leisure Centre
1815-1950

By D. A. DAVIES

Journal 9, 1986

At the present time Bromyard Downs is widely used for open air relaxation by families and individuals for activities ranging from walking the dog to quite elaborate picnic enterprises. To these users and the casual passers-by little evidence is immediately apparent of how the northern end of the Downs was used for organised sport and recreation during the 19th and early 20th centuries. These activities included racing, shooting, golf and bowls, all of which required laid-out physical facilities of considerable extent and it is noteworthy that these were provided within the existing settlement pattern of Norton Township which was largely as we see it today. Most of the present houses on Norton Downs are of late 18th or 19th-century build but some do occupy sites of earlier buildings. In setting the recreational areas, skilful use was made of the layout of the ridge, natural obstacles and resources. This was accompanied by a high degree of social involvement and activity. The social frame-work was supported by a number of inns and public houses, only one of which, the Royal Oak, exists today. There was also a Golf Club House and tuck-shop. The public houses in existence in the 19th century were:

> The Royal Oak
> The Bowling Green Inn
> The Fox
> Robert's Hill (Cider House)
> Sunnyside (reputed)

I have approached the individual facilities in chronological order from their date of foundation and so we will come first to:

THE RACE COURSE

This was laid out at the end of the Napoleonic Wars (contemporary with the Brockhampton Estate wall) and is thought to have been part of the relief work for returning soldiers and people affected by the post-war slump. The races were an annual event much appreciated by supporters from all around the locality and, as transport improved, from further afield drawing spectators from Hereford, Worcester, Stourport and eventually with the growth of the railway system from Birmingham. The race cards appear to have been mixed, with races over fences and hurdles pre-dominating, but provision for some events over the flat. The Race Stewards were decidedly top drawer, with the Marquis of Queensberry and the Earl of Coventry among their number, together with MPs and Masters of Hounds. The race committee upon which organisation and management devolved was made up of local men of substance and standing, including the well-known local names of Walker of Knightwick, Devereux, Cooke and Woodhouse.

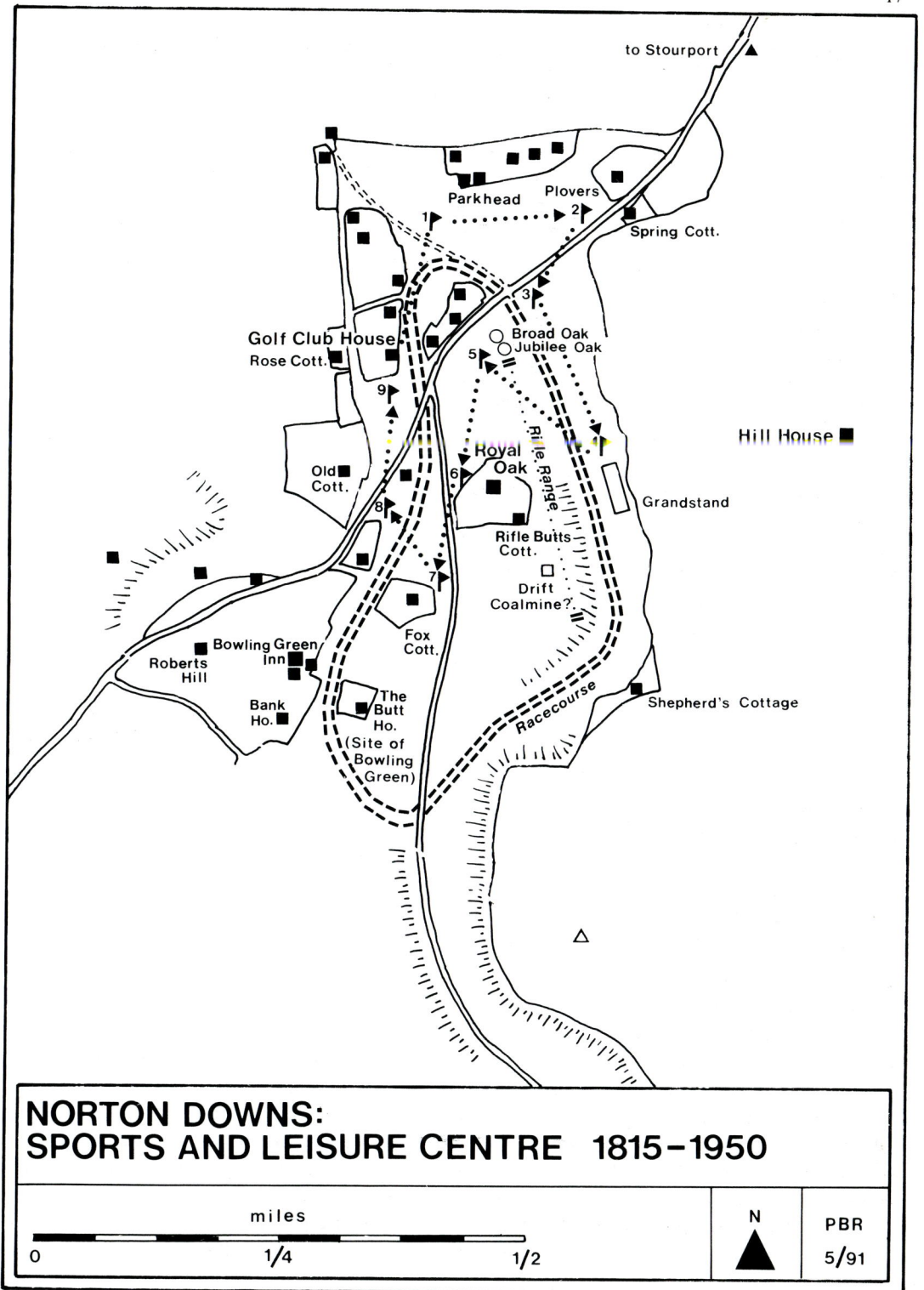

to Stourport

Parkhead

Plovers

1

2

Spring Cott.

3

Broad Oak

Jubilee Oak

Golf Club House

Rose Cott.

5

9

Old Cott.

Royal Oak

Rifle Range

Hill House

6

Grandstand

8

Rifle Butts Cott.

7

Drift Coalmine?

Fox Cott.

Roberts Hill

Bowling Green Inn

Bank Ho.

The Butt Ho. (Site of Bowling Green)

Racecourse

Shepherd's Cottage

NORTON DOWNS:
SPORTS AND LEISURE CENTRE 1815−1950

miles

0   1/4   1/2

N

PBR

5/91

The course itself was laid out with two crossings of the Bromyard - Kidderminster road and one of the Downs road and with a number of jumps, many of which were water jumps each fed from its own pond or spring. These jumps were mainly on the western side of the course below the spring line. Brush for the fences came from the birch coppice at the northern end which extended further on to the common at that time. Members of the Moore family who lived locally were responsible for the construction and maintenance of fences and ditches in the later life of the race course. The course grandstand stood to the east of the present gateway to the Hill House Farm from the Downs and its foundations were visible until the beginning of the Second World War when the site was ploughed up as part of the war effort in agriculture.

The Race Meeting of 1884 attracted some 6,000 to 7,000 spectators and we are fortunate to have a surviving copy of the card for this great day which marked what was probably the apogee of the event. A report in the Ledbury Free Press and Advertiser on the meeting of 1871 shows a similar pattern of racing and states that, 'Fine weather, a large attendance and good sport, left nothing to be desired'.

Change however seemed to be inevitable with the approach and arrival of the 20th century, the race meeting attendances declined, railway excursionists dropped to about 2,000 in 1890 and to 1,500 in 1894. In 1904 the *Bromyard News and Record* noted with regret in its edition of 26th May that the days of race meetings on the course constructed by Bromyard Volunteers at the end of the Napoleonic Wars were to be 'numbered with the past'.

An attempt was made to re-site the race meetings elsewhere in the district but this failed and Bromyard Races were no more, coming to an end at roughly the same time as another Norton Downs usage which had been co-existent for part of the 19th century:

THE RIFLE RANGE

The range ran parallel to the north side of the race course with the 600 yard firing point being just to the east of the Jubilee Oak, and the stop butt being provided by the inner embankment of the race course on its southwards run from the Shepherds Cottage turn. The intermediate firing points at 100 yard intervals along the range can still be traced.

The butts were of mid 19th-century construction and were provided for the 4th Herefordshire Rifle Corps who were raised in the Bromyard area as a result of the tension between Britain and France arising from the foreign policy of Napoleon III in 1859. The adjacent Royal Oak was used for administrative and storage purposes and no doubt for pre- and post-shoot conferences. The target plate of mild steel was seen quite recently and is believed to be lying turf-covered somewhere on the line of the race course embankment. It is likely the first weapons used on this range were the muzzle loading 1853 pattern Enfield rifles which would have given way to Martini-Henry breech loading rifles in the 1870s. The range was established enough to be mentioned in the directories from this period onwards and must have been a well-known feature. Looking at the layout on the ground today one can but wonder at the apparent absence of safety features, and ponder how safe working in the fields of the Warren or in the Warren Wood could have been when the range was in use.

At the time of the Second World War, as mentioned in Ian Buckley's history of Brockhampton School, the pupils there had use of the rifles for drill purposes. It appears that the range became disused in 1905 or shortly thereafter, though whether as a result of greater safety awareness with the advent of higher velocity weapons and ammunition, lack of interest, or the reform of the Volunteers, it is not known. The demise may have been hastened because of incompatibility with the existence of the new sporting facility:

THE GOLF CLUB

Part of whose course overlapped both the rifle range and the race course. It was a nine hole course with a club house, an enthusiastic committee and support staff. The layout of the fairway and greens ran from outside the 'tuck shop' across the Buckenhill Drive toward Park Head Cottages then toward the boundary of Plovers, across the road parallel to the race course as far as the Hill House gate, then to the Jubilee Oak, down to the angle of the Royal Oak hedge and the Downs road then across that road to the green near the Fox, back over the Downs road then towards the Mission Church and back to the final hole in front of the Club House.

The Club was founded around the turn of the century and enjoyed its fullest support between the Wars. During this period Mr. Bert Moore's father who lived at Park Head Cottages was the green-keeper, and Bert has described most graphically the duties that he and his brother had to carry out, before going to school at Brockhampton each morning, to remedy the ravages of sheep on the greens.

Part of the course came under the plough in 1939-40 as part of the War Agricultural Executive Committee's programme to increase food production, and efforts to re-establish and maintain the club post-war failed.

THE BOWLING GREEN

The Bowling Green Inn existed as a public house certainly up to 1920, the actual bowling green was situated inside the race course circuit and the Butt House was built upon it in the mid-1920s. The property of the Bowling Green was held by Richard Mason of Ocle Pychard in the mid-18th century but it had earlier been held on leasehold from the bishop of Hereford. Bowling appears to have been conducted as both a green and alley sport, as there was a reputed alley at Robert's Hill.

Avenbury Church Bells

By JOHN EISEL AND MARIAN HOLBOURN

Journal 8, 1985

During the summer Mr. and Mrs. A. E. Newbold very kindly allowed the Society to make a copy of a photograph of the Avenbury bells. This photograph shows the bells in crates after their removal from the church tower, and prior to their journey to the church of St. Andrew-by-the-Wardrobe in London.

Dr. John Eisel of Ullingswick, the author of *The Church Bells of Hereford Cathedral,* has supplied these notes about the bells.

'These were taken to St. Andrew-by-the-Wardrobe in 1933 and were subsequently blitzed. The two smaller bells, one by Abel Rudhall, 1757, and the other by Ward J. Taylor of Oxford were recast: the largest bell, by the medieval Worcester foundry, was preserved although cracked.

Details of the bells are given in F. Sturge's *Church Bells of Herefordshire* where there is also a photograph. I examined the bell in the early 1960s while a student in London.

This medieval bell is one of a well-known group called ''Royal Head'' bells from the stops used which denote the heads of King Edward III and Queen Philippa. The distribution of known examples suggest that Worcester was the most likely place of casting c1410-20. They are dateable from an example at Bitterley, Shropshire, whose inscription refers to one Alice Sturge who died in 1415. The lettering used (including stop) was formerly in the possession of William Rufford of Toddington, Bedfordshire, who died about 1393.

Avenbury Church, c1843, from a watercolour.

The Royal Head stops remained at Worcester until the Reformation, then were used at Nottingham from c1580-1620, then on a few bells cast in Nottingham at the end of the 18th century and finally were used in 1805 on bells cast by John Briant of Hertford for Waltham Abbey.

The 1757 Rudhall bell is listed in the 1804 Rudhall list.

The church of St. Andrew by-the-Wardrobe has been restored and is now used by the Redundant Churches Fund as their headquarters and there the medieval bell may still be seen.'

Avenbury
Church 1987.

Avenbury Church for long has had a reputation of being haunted by music and by the bells. Be that as it may we reproduce here part of a letter published in the 1950s in the *Bromyard News and Record* written by Mrs. Marian Holbourn. We leave you to draw your own conclusions!

'Avenbury Church had three beautiful bells, one of which bore a Latin inscription meaning "I am Gabriel, messenger from Heaven". As the church was dedicated to St. Mary, the name of the bell doubtless commemorated the archangel's annunciation to the Virgin. The other bells were named, if I remember rightly, Paul and Andrew, but Gabriel was the master. He was the passing bell and his tolling aided the departing soul and accompanied the body on its last journey to the grave. He was said to toll of his own accord when a vicar died or when tragedy affected the Parish.

I was living in Scotland when my father died. He had a seizure in church and was carried home on a stretcher. He lived on for 10 days and as his end was not thought to be imminent I was not sent for in time to see him alive. Our daily help, Sarah, lamented that I had not been summoned earlier. "They said they did not know he was dying", she exclaimed indignantly. "But they knew perfectly well that bell never tolls for nothing!'' She said that the bell started tolling about nine o'clock in the evening and that it wakened her several times during the night. Sarah was deaf and we always had to shout into her ear but she heard the bell distinctly.

I shall never forget Gabriel's peculiarly deep tone as my father's coffin was carried from the church where he had ministered for 34 years. The first stroke of the great bell sent a shudder down my spine. Within the sound there seemed to be a voice, an undertone of awful solemnity and warning.

During the days that followed every member of the family confessed to imagining that they heard the bell tolling. But, except for my mother, we were conscious that it was subjective, coming from within. Every morning when I went to her room Mother told me she had been unable to sleep because of ''that bell, tolling, tolling, tolling all through the night''. It affected her health so that I had to hurry my arrangements to take her away from the house.

My father the Rev. E. H. Archer-Shepherd, was the last vicar of Avenbury. The Parish was divided between three neighbouring ones; the church was dismantled and the bells sold to a London church with the curious name, St. Andrew-by-the-Wardrobe. Our aged sexton was almost beside himself. ''If you sell the bells'', he warned, ''a curse will fall upon the Parish''.

And what of the sorrowing Gabriel. During the London blitz the church where the bells hung was destroyed. I passed the site and could find not one stone to indicate that a church had ever stood on the spot. Later I learned to my great joy that the bells were saved.'

Reprinted from the "Hereford Times," Dec. 22nd, 1917.

THE MISSING PEARL,

OR

FAR ABOVE RUBIES.

By the Rev. E. H. Archer-Shepherd, M.A.,

Vicar of Avenbury, Bromyard.

Founded partly on the Arabian Night's story, "Prince Zeyn Alasnam and the King of the Genii," and partly upon the lines of Dryden :—

" Clytorean streams the love of wine expel,
  (Such is the virtue of the abstemious well),
Whether the colder nymph that rule the
    flood,
Extinguishes and balks the drunken god ;
Or that Melampus (so have some assured),
When the mad Praetides with charms he
    cured,
And powerful herbs, both charms and
    simples cast
Into the sober spring, where still their
    virtues last."

The Stone Road at Jumper's Hole

By MILDRED SHEPHERD

Newsletter 2, 1971

We have received a most interesting letter from Miss Joan Hatton of Hereford, who in the 1940s visited Stanford Bishop a great deal. She speaks of an ancient track that traverses the parish. She says, 'A vestige of the ancient track is to be found on the Whelpley Brook which forms the boundary between the parishes of Acton Beauchamp and Stanford Bishop. The spot is known as Jumper's Hole, where the bed of the little stream is paved with unworked slabs of water-worn stone, one of which is pierced with a rounded hole... The name Stanford may therefore mean Stan = stone, ford from the Welsh fordd, a road — the stone road.'

Miss Hatton also says, 'In connection with Jumper's Hole the following folk story is told, ''A woman stole a loaf of bread from Stanford Bishop. She mounted her horse and galloped away down the hill. She came to the brook and as the horse jumped, the loaf fell from her basket on to a stone and there is the dent to this day''. That Stanford-on-Teme is connected with Stanford Bishop is apparent from a similar story concerning a stolen mare whose hoof marks were visible on the stones as she galloped along the bed of the Sapey Brook.' She also says, 'That the stone road led southward into Herefordshire is probable, since this folk-tale crops up again with St. Katherine riding the stolen mare on her entry into Ledbury.'

The above interested me so much that this summer I have been over twice to Stanford Bishop to see it as it is now. I also asked the Rector and the farmer on whose land Jumper's Hole is, and collected two variations of the folk-story, one that an old couple after shopping in Bromyard dropped a loaf as they crossed the brook and this caused the hole. The other, that as the horse jumped the brook it put its foot on the stone and caused the hole - just about the same as the Stanford-on-Teme legend. These legends crop up all over the country and began in very early ages when people were groping for an explanation of something they could not understand.

Studying various maps, it does look as though foot-paths, bridle paths and stretches of road if joined up could lead north to Stanford-on-Teme, and also south to Ledbury. The ancient track is very clear through Stanford Bishop west of the church drive. I was able to walk a short way on it though most of it is badly overgrown now. Down the two sloping meadows it has become merged with the meadows, with the one hedge-side left which is a boundary hedge.

Miss Hatton remarks on the circular shape of the Stanford Bishop churchyard, which shows it was a holy place in early ages before Christianity. She also mentions the standing stone to the right of the gateway to the churchyard. This may well be one of the ancient circle stones as it is on the periphery of the circle. It is at present hidden by holly in a tall mixed hedge.

The crossing-place on the brook is made of natural rocks, of which there are a number about, and consists of three flat boulders, one of which has the hole in it. There is no evidence of the stone setts put at fords of the Middle Ages to help the packhorses keep a foothold crossing and up the banks.

I should think myself that with so many factors pointing to it, that Miss Hatton has told us of one of the earliest tracks in the district, one probably connecting with the Acton Beauchamp saltway mentioned by Professor G. B. Grundy.

12mC. Church. Castle Frome.

Castle Frome

By K. A. LINDSAY

Newsletter 5, 1973

As a newcomer to this district, I was very impressed by the amount of historical interest in this small out-of-the-way spot.

Castle Frome, which is referred to on old maps as Frome of the Castle or Frome of the King, is about two miles from Bishops Frome and about the same distance from Canon Frome, which received its name from the canons of Llanthony Abbey who administered it. The river Frome skirts the above villages and runs through Bromyard. The old canal runs south-west of Canon Frome towards Hereford and became disused after the railway was built.

In 1645 during the Civil War, a Scottish army, under the Earl of Leven, attempted to capture Hereford for the Parliamentarians; failing to do this the Scots infiltrated round Hereford and reached the Frome valley. There was a royalist garrison at Canon Frome where there was a residence belonging to the Hopton family, with a drawbridge and moat. It was a strategic point in the line of communication between Hereford and Worcester, and changed hands on several occasions. A most interesting account of these operations is contained in the *Military Memoir of Colonel Birch,* which can be found in the Herefordshire County Library.

The castle, from which Castle Frome gets its name, was situated on high ground east of the church; it is reputed to have been destroyed in the Stephen and Matilda wars and today only the remnants of its earthworks survive in thick woodlands. Town Farm, close to the church is not particularly old, but excavations have revealed Roman roadworks and specimens of wild hellebore which is a sign of Roman occupation.

The church of St. Michael is small, but well constructed and maintained; there is a sunken roadway running just north of the church towards the castle. The most interesting features of the church of St. Michael are the Unett tomb, the font, the stone crusader's head, and the communion chalice; these will be described later. Inside the churchyard there is a magnificent yew tree about nine feet in diameter, while the local Gospel Yew is near the lodge to Birchend about one mile away on the Ledbury road.

There are various Gospel yews, oaks and ashes scattered about the country, where the local parsons used to hold occasional services. At the Birchend one there was a seat where farmers used to gather in the evening for a chat.

Birchend was the seat of the Unett family and the lodge is a very colourful Victorian landmark with gay gardens on the road to Ledbury, built by a Mr Pitt of Birchend for his lady-love. This practice seems to have been a common one in these parts, because I have been told that the owner of Paunton Court did the same thing in Victorian times. Not much is known of the original Birchend building which was burnt down at some time, but there was a homestead moat, which was destroyed at the time of the modernization of the farm.

Mrs. Farr, who lives at Yarkhill now, lived at Castle Frome most of her life, and was able to provide me with local information. She says her mother told her that one lady of the village used to avoid paying toll at the turnpike by driving her donkey-cart down the front drive of Birchend and up the back to rejoin the road.

The name Unett is not a common one and there are no apparent descendants in this neighbourhood, but Mr John Unett of Malvern has carried out considerable research and has produced a family tree which hangs on the church wall, together with a black and white reproduction of the two figures on the Unett tomb. Old records show that in 1569 the manor was leased to William Unett for the term of 10,000 years at the yearly rent of one red rose. Mr John Unett claims no descent from this family, but from a Staffordshire branch. The Unetts married into various local families but not with the Slaughters of Cheyney Court, the other big house in the neighbourhood which was also burnt down, the only remains being a 16th-century barn, said to have been used as a chapel, with an interesting turret. The heroine of *In Spite of All* a novel by Edna Lyall (1901) describing Herefordshire during the Civil Wars, was one Hilary Unett.

The Unett Tomb.

The Mormon connection with Castle Frome is rather an extraordinary one. In 1840 John Benbow, who farmed Hill Farm, joined the Latter Day Saints and taking with him about 600 converts went to Salt Lake City, U.S.A., where he became a leading member of the community. An old man, William Taylor, who died some forty years ago, aged about eighty, worked all his life at Hill Farm and was told by his parents how John Benbow had organised the United Brethren and how they were all baptised in a pond a short distance from Hill House. For many years, with the exception of the war years, a steady trickle of Mormon pilgrims came in August and September. After the last war, owing to the American forces being over here, they came all the year round. They came to see the pond and occasionally a child was baptised. On the whole they were harmless types, dressed like black crows, and some were interested in the church registers to trace their ancestors. One unfortunate local man lost his good-looking wife, who was smuggled off to the U.S.A. and not heard of since. There are three Benbows buried in Castle Frome churchyard. Ann aged 95 in 1851, Sarah aged 69 in 1855 and Thomas aged 80 in 1873.

Returning to the church of St. Michael, which was built in the 12th century, it was restored in 1878, and the black and white bell turret and porch were tastefully constructed, unlike so many Victorian reproductions of that period. There are three bells, one inscribed 'MAUDILLAMOR'. There is an old sundial over the main entrance which was obviously erected before the porch was built; the black and white belfry is quite a landmark. The communion silver is valuable, the chalice dates back to 1571. The north wall of the nave is an interesting example of 12th-century masonry.

The Unett tomb, with alabaster reclining figures of a cavalier and his wife, is situated in the sanctuary and includes small effigies of his family. An interesting mystery is the fact that four daughters are represented on the tomb, but only three are referred to on the tablet overhead.

A stone effigy which is likely to be missed by visitors is a crusader's bust in chain mail holding a casket. It obviously contained the heart of a knight killed in Palestine, where his body was buried.

The outstanding treasure of the church is the ancient stone font, reputed to be Norman, but the carving has a Scandinavian influence and represents the four evangelistic creatures and the Baptism. It is very similar to the Tympanum in Fownhope Church which shows the Virgin and Child, eagle and lion.

The monuments have not been unduly knocked about, but Mrs. Unett's nose has caught it, and the East window has had to be replaced; some of the mediaeval glass has been preserved on the south side of the church.

The new East window was erected in memory of Lieut. Raine, R.E., who was killed in France in 1918. His parents lived at Hanburies, Bishops Frome, but preferred to worship at Castle Frome Church. The latest memorial in the church is a tasteful black and gold tablet to Lieut. Lock of Paunton Court, who was killed at Alamein.

Cheyney Court Mansion

By H. H. R. MOILLIET

Journal 7, 1984

Cheyney Court Mansion was for many years the residence of the late Mr. T. Cook, whose family is well known in Bromyard. In or about the year 1866 the mansion was purchased by the late Mr James Moilliet, who built a north wing and made other extensive alterations. Mr Moilliet was a gentleman of wealth, derived from an interest in a London bank. He was known as the squire and made a beneficent exercise of his position. One room in the house was set apart for treats for the villagers and schoolchildren. Mr Moilliet was a gentleman of bookish inclinations, who did not go much into society, or engage actively in business. His son, Captain H. H. R. Moilliet, R.I.M., left some notes about Cheyney Court in the middle of the 19th century, which we are able to reproduce here.

'The Mansion was a monastery - a small one - dating from the fourteenth century. We have a spur, with a wicked spiked rowel, reckoned to be a fourteenth-century one, which was dug up, together with a skull, in the stable yard. Two of the ancient rooms I remember: the Old Hall, oak floored and panelled, and the room above it, which was the old monks' refectory, and had a small annexe opening off it for the abbot, with a blue domed roof with angels painted on it. I do not know how many rooms there were, but my mother said she could put up twenty guests, though some of the bedrooms were very small, for visitors' servants. In those days if one gave a dinner party to, say, six couples, half of them, who might live some miles away, would probably have to spend the night out. ''Where I dines I sleeps,'' as John Jorrocks said. Accommodation was accordingly required for five or six horses and several coachmen, footmen, and a lady's maid or two.

My grandfather, James Moilliet, built a new front to the house, of white freestone, which did not fit in with the old building.

My mother employed six women servants (no butler), and another six came to the big laundry room weekly to do the household washing. We also had six gardeners, a coachman (Dains, a wonderful man with horses, and a very great friend), one or two grooms, and a cowman who looked after the four or five cows which supplied milk to the house and also looked after the poultry, luggage cart, and cob. (When a lady came on a visit, if only for the week-end, she brought a four-foot domed-top trunk and several boxes, so that a light two-wheeled cart and a stout cob were essential.) The garden was large and wild (a lovely playground), with three tennis courts and a two-acre kitchen garden with three greenhouses.

The farm was worked by Mr Bishop and his sons, and much later by Mr Eli who, it was said, never missed a running rabbit with his hammer muzzle-loader.

We kept five horses: a pair for the landau, the luggage-cart cob, our dear Welsh pony Polly (on whom we all learnt to ride, so far as a very small boy can), and our wonderful Bluegrass, a Canadian trotter who was the fastest horse in the district. He drew a very

Cheyney Court Mansion in 1872.

light four-wheeled hickory-built buggy. He carried his nose level with his ears, and once knocked my Dad's pipe out of his mouth, when Dad was riding him, with his ears. He was never touched with the whip - rattle it in its socket, and Bluegrass was off at speed. Dad would never put a martingale on him: "He's proud of himself, and I'm proud of him; let him carry his head as he likes." We loved all our horses, and after church on Sundays we all went round the stables with lumps of sugar or carrots, and Dains enjoyed it with us, and the horses whinnied.

I look back on my Cheyney days with great pleasure, but my mother was not so happy: she knew that Dad had to spend capital to keep it going.

The roads were bad. Coarse metal was spread and wagon tyres and horses' hooves had to work it in. The first steam roller, Invicta, appeared in (I think) 1886: what a wonderful improvement it made - and how it frightened the horses!

The Frome overflowed every winter, and I remember ferrying people in the pony cart who were stuck on the crown of a bridge, with two feet of rushing water in front and behind. The red clay mud in winter was something awful. Picking my way with my Dad to church one day, I remember I saw a nice clean billycock on the mud near a ditch. Of course I got across and picked it up. The head under it said "I'm very glad to see you, Mr Moilliet, I was getting anxious. Will you please call in at the farm just along and ask them to help me out of the mud - and my horse which is under me!"

Some social customs obtained then which were curious. When my mother, as a young married woman, went out to dinner, she must always take with her a liveried footman. All he did was to stand against the wall behind her chair at dinner. "You see, my dear," said Mother, "Gentlemen often drank too much at dinner, so his duty was to help his mistress if her partner became obstreperous."

My Father, though a comparatively poor man, with little land, was the Squire, which meant something then. The Squire, the Parson, and the Doctor - if there was a resident one - more or less ran the village, and pretty well they did it, while the Squire's lady was of course the unpaid District Nurse.

"The old order changeth, giving place to new," but I seem to remember a warm friendliness then which I do not find very often now.'

The Sibyls' Room

'The room is thirty feet long by twenty feet wide, oak panelled, with a series of curious paintings in the upper compartments, representing thirteen Sibyls and eighteen Prophets - a strange mixture of the sacred and profane which has its climax above the fine Tudor fireplace, where are placed in juxta-position pictures of the goddess Diana and St. John the Baptist. The latter is represented contemplating the Lamb of God, and the picture is inscribed with the words *Ecce Agnus ille Dei, Qui tollit peccata mundi;* beneath the portraits of the Sibyls are appropriate legends, and although neither the poetic or pictorial skill exhibited is remarkable the general effect is very good.'

The drawings and the above note are taken from *A History of the Mansions and Manors of Herefordshire* (1872) by the Rev. C. J. Robinson.

With the removal of the Moilliet family to Malvern, Cheyney Court was let to Mr. Alfred John Monson. By this time Cheyney Court had become a country seat commodious enough for a gentleman of moderate social ambition. A suite of stables adjoined the house, the grounds were laid out with a small lake, a fountain, a terrace and the artificial elegances common to country residences. At the time Mr. Moilliet let the house he stipulated for a room in which he might store his plate and some furniture, pictures and some valuable books.

The new tenant at Cheyney Court proved to be a gentleman of breeding, manners and education. His wife was a young and prepossessing woman. They had one child. A considerable establishment was set up. Four women servants were kept - nurse, cook, housemaid, scullerymaid. The household also included a butler, a page boy and one or two gardeners were kept at various times. Six or seven pupils (probably agricultural) also enlarged the establishment, but for these, of course, Monson was paid. There were two or three of twelve or fourteen years of age, a couple aged about seventeen or eighteen and one aged 23 or 25. They lived well of course, as was to be expected of the sons of wealthy fathers.

For the eldest of these pupils Mr. Monson is said to have received £200 a year. One kept a hunter. Either Mr. Monson or the pupils between them kept a pack of harriers to the indignation of some of the neighbouring residents over whose land the dogs occasionally found their way. It is estimated by the neighbourhood that the expenses of the establishment must have run to a couple of thousand a year. Mr. Monson did not visit much in the County. He was not in fact, there long enough to establish himself in societies. He rode well at hunt, and kept four or five horses. He had not been there long when a hayrick was burned down. Happily the policy of insurance had been sent to him only a short time before so that the loss was covered.

A second fire occurred not very long after in the butler's pantry. This was supposed to have been occasioned by the accidental ignition of some paraffin. It was discovered before it had made much headway.

A few yards from the house is a very fine suite of stables. Early on the morning of the 1st July 1887, the stables were observed to be on fire. The place is not far from the village, and a crowd at once got round. Messengers were sent for the neighbouring fire brigades, and in the meantime the villagers began pouring water on the flames with the implements they had at hand. Suddenly the discovery was made that the horses were in the stables, and that the door was locked. Mr. Monson appears to have forgotten this, until one of the residents in the village shouted out to him *'WHY THE DEVIL DON'T YOU LOOSE THE HORSES?'*. Monson made some reply inaudible amidst the uproar attending the conflagration. The villagers, taking the initiative, got axes and heavy weapons, with which they battered open the doors and the poor animals were released. It was fortunate that they were, or they would inevitably have been roasted or burned to death. The stables were burned out. Much surprise was expressed that Mr Monson should have forgotten to unlock the doors, but of course sufficient excuse may not have been made for his condition under the excitement of the moment. The horses were insured by Mr. Monson in the Hand-in-Hand Fire Office, and the building by Mr. Moilliet in the Caledonian.

Cheyney Court Mansion, Serious Fire Near Bromyard. Destruction of Cheyney Court
27 July 1888

One of the most disastrous of fires, that have occurred lately, and which neither time nor money can replace, was the burning of Cheyney Court, near Bishop's Frome, on Tuesday morning last.

The fire was first seen about 5.30 in the morning by a man going to work, and was supposed to have originated from an incubator in the library. The family left the house the day previously, leaving by the 5 o'clock train from Bromyard. The butler was left in charge and was sleeping in the house, being aroused only just in time to escape in his night apparel, and then having to pass through fire and smoke. The Bromyard engine (under the captaincy of Mr McIntosh) was first on the spot, shortly followed by the Ledbury fire brigade; and in a lapse of 20 minutes the second Ledbury brigade arrived. It was evident on the arrival of the engines that the fire had got too good a hold for the front of the house to be saved, and all attention was directed to the other parts of the building as yet intact. Supt. Ovens did admirable work with a small garden hose, which he attached to a water pipe in the back-kitchen, keeping the fire from a back wing of the house, and thus preventing it from spreading to the stables, which, it will be remembered were burnt down last year. At 9 o'clock in the morning the house (except a few back offices) was completely

The firefighters.

gutted. The debris was then smoking, and firemen were playing on different parts of the ruins that were still burning. A large water tank situated on the top of the house and supported by beams which were on fire, was seen to be gradually giving way. There were large cracks in the walls of the new portion of the house, and at intervals portions of the structure were still falling with loud crashes. It was noticed the fire expended itself on the middle and front of the house, and that the sides and back were not so much damaged owing no doubt to the wind, which was blowing N.E. at the time.

It was very lucky that the fire occurred when it did, for had it occurred 48 hours before the possibility is that Mr. and Mrs. Monson and the servants would have been in great danger. On Monday morning most of the servants had, according to previous notice received, left the house. Mrs. Monson at the same time left for London. Late on Monday evening the butler drove Mr. Monson to Ledbury Station, and returned to the Court. He went, according to his own subsequent account, through the house and saw nothing that looked in any way dangerous. Then he went to bed and was only aroused by the stones which came through the window.

There was just one agent to which the fire was attributed. An incubator in use was left in the library, and it is supposed that this became overheated, and so started the fire. With the exception of two or three servants' rooms and the kitchen quarter, the building was quite burned out. Hardly anything could be saved from the fire.

Mr. Moilliet's belongings, his plate, pictures and furniture were all burned and destroyed in the great conflagration. So thoroughly had the fire performed its work of destruction that hardly anything was recovered from the ashes that were riddled. The diamonds and jewellery that Mrs. Monson left behind her are also perished.

In some quarters the suggestion of incendiarism was made; but no proof was forthcoming that the fire was anything but an accident. The building was insured by Mr. Moilliet for £4,000; his effects which were stored in one of the rooms were insured for £1,500, and £650 stood opposite the pictures in Mr. Moilliet's policy, but some of these Mr. Moilliet had taken to his new residence several miles away.

Mr. Monson's furniture was insured for £2,000.

The Bromyard News, 2.8.1888

Alfred Monson was later to be accused of the murder of a student, in what became known as the Ardliament mystery. The Scottish court brought in a verdict of Not Proven, but one may imagine how the case must have caused tongues to wag along the Frome valley.

German Gypsies On Tour

"They Pass Through Bromyard Causing Great Excitement"

Supt. Lewis received information on Wednesday morning that a large number of German Gypsies were making their way to Bromyard from Hereford and from information received from the latter town the Super warned all shopkeepers to take in all their goods that were exhibited outside and to keep a sharp lookout. When all the police in the district gathered and proceeded towards Hereford work practically stopped in Bromyard. The reports also of their numbers were enlarged from time to time and their doings in Hereford. It was felt that the local Volunteers should be called out to defend the town.

The police came upon the gypsies encamped near Burley Gate Post Office. There were nine to a dozen men and some twenty women and children. They were persuaded "in a friendly manner" to go on to Worcester, where there was a Horse Fair. They eventually reached Bromyard about 4 o'clock. They were very amiable the chief grievance being that the children were continually asking for pennies. They encamped for the night on the Worcester road by the Stream Hall Works.

Bromyard News & Record, 30.8.1906

Gypsies c1892.

Herb Growing at Stoke Lacy 1939 - 1989

By MADGE HOOPER

Journal 11, 1988

It was the end of 1939 and the war was going through that early 'phoney' period. Hitler's dreaded invasion had not materialised and in country districts life went on much as before.

In Stoke Lacy, more disturbing than the war was the severing of the last link with the Morgan family. Prebendary Henry Morgan, who with his father had held the incumbency for 65 years, had died in 1936. His unmarried daughter, Dorothy, had decided to leave the parish rather than live in Stoke House, which had been built for her in 1934. For generations the Morgan family had deeply influenced and shaped the lives of the people of Stoke Lacy and without them the parish was rather like a ship without a rudder.

The building of Stoke House had been a matter of much interest locally - the first new house for decades. It had been occupied by Mr. Morgan's curate and then two short-term tenants, but in 1939 it was again To Let.

My husband, Robert, and I had searched country-wide for a suitable property with a small parcel of land attached. One viewing was sufficient to convince us that Stoke House and its 6½ acres of land was exactly what we wanted. It seemed appropriate that we should develop our Herb Farm on what had been known for many years as Flower Show Meadow.

The annual Stoke Lacy Flower Show was a prestigious affair in the county and competition was keen to present the finest flowers, fruit and vegetables. Races and sideshows made the day an eventful and exciting one, much looked forward to by all in the neighbourhood. It was sad that the war and change of circumstances had to put an end to this successful and happy annual highlight.

When Flower Show Meadow was ploughed over it was not surprising that our neighbours wondered what we were up to! The Ministry of Agriculture were issuing directives about suitable farm and horticultural crops and we appeared to be planting the land with 'a lot of old weeds'! The Min. of Ag. were, in fact, also encouraging the growing of culinary and medicinal herbs to replace those which had previously been imported from the continent. A little later when the Women's Institutes throughout the country were asked to co-operate in the collecting of vital wild herbs our 'old weeds' started to be taken seriously.

I had completed my training and had had four years experience of herb growing, drying and processing in Kent before coming to Herefordshire, so I was able to travel around the W.I.s in this and surrounding counties explaining which herbs were needed, advising at what stage they should be gathered and showing how to dry them. We collected much of this material from the Institutes and sent it off in bulk to manufacturing chemists. Older members will remember collecting rose hips which would supply, in syrup, the much needed vitamin C for young children and expectant mothers. Other herbs were elder-flowers, yarrow, agrimony and foxglove leaves and seeds, important for the digitalin they would yield, valuable for the treatment of some heart complaints.

The soil in Kent had been sandy and light and it drained quickly so that one could soon resume work after heavy rain. The red Herefordshire clay was a whole new experience! The first spring - and in many subsequent ones - we wondered if the soil would ever 'come to hand'. For weeks after the accustomed planting time in Kent the Herefordshire soil resembled plasticine. If trodden or worked when wet it padded down and drying winds would turn it into tiles or bricks. But we could see what a lush county Herefordshire was and the success attained by local gardeners encouraged us. We kept our eyes and ears open and learned that nothing was to be gained by being too impatient to cultivate in early spring. The advice given by one wise old local sage was 'You've got to learn to humour it, and never put your hoe down''. And that in a nutshell was the secret of it.

The land was divided into plantations of different sizes to grow perennial crops of thyme - some of which went to food manufacturers and some to manufacturing chemists to produce thymol for use in cold and cough medicines; sage and marjoram - favourite herbs for stuffing and sausages; savory and mint - all making the restricted wartime diet more palatable. Tarragon was grown for the vinegar works in Worcester. These plantations could be harvested twice and sometimes three times a year for five or six years.

While the herbs were getting established we grew vegetables for a private school evacuated to the Rectory, but there were problems other than the texture of the soil. The ploughed-in pasture was full of wireworm and the brook bank, undisturbed for years, was riddled with rabbit warrens. As we planted, so the rabbits cleared and eventually we had to sink wire netting around the whole area. Later on myxomatosis eliminated the rabbits and in due course naphthalene won the battle with the wireworm.

One part of the land was devoted to growing urgently needed drug plants - deadly nightshade *(Atropa Belladonna)*, henbane *(Hyoscyamus niger)*, thornapple *(Datura stramonium)* and monkshood *(Aconitum napellus)*. To produce the highest yield of the constituent required it was important that they were harvested with attention given to the correct stage of their development and the necessary part of the plant - it could be root, leaves and/or stem, or seed.

Red roses and marigolds *(Calendula officinalis)* were grown for medicinal use and where possible selected flowers were planted and dried and made into pot pourri which, when exported to America, earned some dollars for Britain.

As we cultivated over the land we discovered buried 'treasure'! When we turned over the very first root of new potatoes there emerged a George III coin, and other coins, obviously dropped during the many years of merry-making on Flower Show Meadow, came to light.

The herbs fall into a natural sequence to be cut for drying. Thyme was always the first crop and when all the other herbs had been harvested the second crop of thyme would soon be ready to set the process in motion again. A special drying shed had been erected. The windows were blacked-out so that the herbs would keep their colour while drying. The heat was provided by a Tortoise slow-combustion coke stove and the herbs were spread on trays of hessian on wire racks and had to be turned daily to ensure even drying. When dry they were either packed into sacks with leaf on stalk or rubbed through sieves to eliminate the stalks to produce a clean, finely broken leaf for culinary use. Roots and seeds were cleaned or washed before drying. The tarragon was cut and stacked in a cool place until it was collected by lorry and taken in its fresh state to Worcester. Fine weather was vital for this operation and there was much finger-crossing and fervent praying!

At last the war ended and before long it became obvious that many of the crops would no longer be economically worth growing, as imports from abroad trickled in and when the trickle swelled to a steady flow the prices fell.

One of the most pressing needs of the post-war period was the building of new houses. Houses meant gardens and gardens began to mean herbs. At first people sought a few essential cooking herbs - 'the faithful four', thyme, parsley, mint and sage; then some old favourites for their sweet scents - lavender, rosemary, old man and then, with a new concept of garden planning, interest was shown in the wide variety of attractive foliage plants - red sage, golden lemon balm and the silver artemisias (relatives of old man).

As supplies of foodstuffs became more readily available a renewed interest in cooking replaced the can-opener and in due course holidays abroad replaced annual visits to a favoured seaside resort. French, Spanish and Italian dishes became familiar and naturally they and the herbs they used were experimented with in the home kitchen.

So the Herb Farm experienced its first change of direction. Where there had been plantations of drug plants and some herbs for bulk drying, young nursery stock was propagated and grown on to supply the need for retail plant sales. At first the lifting time for plants was spring and autumn and most of the business was mail order to any part of the country and to many places abroad. Then came the most revolutionary period in the history of horticulture - the garden centre was born. Plants were container-grown or 'containerised' and an 'instant garden', which appealed to many people who had been caught up in the 'dig for victory' drive, could quickly replace cabbages and potatoes with roses, herbaceous plants, herbs and shrubs.

The media greeted herbs with enthusiasm. Much was made of the 'olde worlde charme', of their folklore and 'magic' and reporters and producers trod a path to the Herb Farm and concocted articles and programmes, good, bad and indifferent. An increasing demand was made for talks on all aspects of herbs and their uses. 'The old weeds' came into their own again when the Ministry of Defence commissioned me to give lectures to H.M. Forces on the value of wild plants as food and for simple medicinal purposes in survival circumstances. At that time I received some quaint looks from those who thought that taxpayers' money could be better spent than employing me to enlarge on the virtues of nettles and dandelions!

Agricultural and Horticultural Shows were re-establishing themselves throughout the country and we travelled the circuit. They were hard work, but interesting and friendly and the herb stands always attracted a good deal of attention.

The public was beginning to want to see where the herbs were grown and the time had come to open the herb farm to visitors. Many groups came for evening visits and each year was fully booked for talks to organisations of all types.

A tearoom was opened and for five years served guests and visitors to the garden with home-made fare and sold home-made preserves, herb jellies, etc.

The time came when another change of direction was indicated and Stoke House was sold. A bungalow and new garden took shape on part of the land no longer used for growing herbs and the propagation of plants for sale was intensified. Some land was let to a local farmer and it was thought fitting that the enterprise should be renamed Stoke Lacy Herb Garden. After 40 years it was decided that travelling about to give talks was no longer practicable, but as an alternative half-day herb schools were arranged at the herb garden during the summer months.

Over the years the garden continued to evolve. One nursery area was cleared and encouraged to become natural woodland, helped along with a little tree planting. Some years later the other nursery was redesigned with shrubs and small trees on grass and identification beds laid out, grouping families of plants together and making a more attractive layout for visitors - who are welcome to come into the garden and wander or sit and enjoy the small peaceful oasis.

The remark must have been made several times a year since we came to Stoke Lacy that 'herbs are getting much more popular'. They have been getting more popular since prehistoric times! They provided food, medicine, fabrics and dyes when, apart from animals, few other sources were known. The distribution of herbs from continent to continent and the survival of these remarkable plants makes an enthralling saga.

Readers of *The Clan of the Cave Bear* will recall Isa's use of chamomile, willow bark, marigolds and elecampane. It is a homely thought that papyrus found in early Egyptian tombs gave recipes to prevent the hair turning grey, for stomach upsets and 'nerves' - all using herbs. Perhaps the first practice of holistic medicine was when the Greeks took their sick to the temples to treat them with healing herbs and soothe them with sweet music in beautiful and peaceful surroundings.

When the monks laid out their formal physic gardens with herbs to treat the ailments of their order and those who came from outside for help - was not this an early example of community care?

Not all herbal cures were pleasant. Hasn't there always been a claim that the nastier the taste the better the medicine? One Gilbertus Anglicus, the author of a successful compendium of medicine is celebrated for

GILBERT'S PUPPY DOG OINTMENT

'Take a very fat puppy dog and skin him, then take the juice of wild cucumber, rue, pellitory, ivy and juniper berries, euphorbium, castoreum; fat of vulture, fox, goose and bear in equal parts; stuff the puppy therewith then boil him; add wax to the grease that floats on the surface and make an ointment.'

It is good to know that nowadays research is taking the place of conjecture into the potential good of herbs. It is not unreasonable to believe that if the poisonous drug plants have played an important role in orthodox medicine there must be enormous scope for good in the beneficial herbs growing in many parts of the world. Already common 'weeds' have gained recognition - e.g. feverfew *(Chrysanthemum Parthenium)* in the treatment of migraine; evening primrose *(Oenothera biennis)* the oil of which yields gamma linolenic acid used for tension problems; elecampane *(Inula Helenium)* - linked in folklore with Helen of Troy, who was said to be gathering it when she was carried off by Paris - has been assessed by the World Food Organisation for its possible use in Third World countries.

Growing herbs for fifty years has been a rich and colourful experience. Inevitably there have been flies in the herbal ointment! Being described as a herbalist rather than a herb grower has led to a good deal of confusion. An over-enthusiastic journalist can start a flood of letters and visits from people who want to believe that 'the magic of herbs' can work miracles. Sometimes just taking time to listen to what people want to talk about, followed by a gentle suggestion that commonsense is better than magic can send them away happier than when they came!

Herbs have opened doors for me, have sent me on exciting journeys to America and New Zealand; they have given me friends worldwide and enjoyment beyond measure. Herefordshire is a county well-blessed with wild herbs - we should do all we can to protect them.

Prebendary Henry Morgan and Dorothy in a Morgan car (see page 36). The first Morgan cars were developed at Stoke Lacy Rectory before the business moved to Malvern.

My Walk Down Memory Lane With Pencombe School

By EDITH E. JONES

Journal 8, 1985

It brings back nostalgic memories when I look back over the years connected with Pencombe School. I remember my own school days, a very happy time for me.

Our Headmaster was Mr. Waldron and his wife was infant teacher, they lived in the school house. Mr. Waldron was a very upright tall soldierly figure, on the other hand Mrs. Waldron was short with a cosy figure. She always dressed in beautiful striped silk dresses of Macclesfield silk to suit herself. They were a very happy family, Of course it was quite a strict discipline in those days and very little surplus furniture in the classrooms.

The main things in the infant room I remember were the blackboard, a large wicker-work sewing container and a stand with large beads for the infants to count.

Mrs. Waldron taught the girls sewing and knitting, she was excellent at both, in fact I used to sit sometimes entranced as the knitting needles seemed to be almost a mere flash. Mrs. Waldron used to give us a thorough training in knitting and needle work. With sewing we first learned to hem correctly on small pieces of material, we then began by making ironholders with a loop on the one corner. We then graduated to making nightdresses, aprons, etc. Everything had firstly to be pinned and then tacked. We often did embroidery work on the garments - designs that had been transferred on in flowers and the like. We usually worked this in Clarke's Silko. I am afraid I never had a flair for needle work but funnily enough Mrs. Waldron often held my hemming up as an example of neat stitching. I was always agreeably surprised about this.

She was a very good infant teacher. Mr. Waldron said on more than one occasion the grounding she gave the pupils was a great help to him later on.

We also had another teacher, she used to take what we called standard two and three as they followed on from the infants. Her name was Miss Hodges and she cycled from the Ullingswick area daily. All she had was a blackboard in front of the class and I am sure if I remember rightly that she did not have a chair to sit down.

Mr. Waldron taught up the other end of the classroom, he was quite strict. If you wanted to leave the room you raised your arm first to ask permission, if he did not happen to notice that was just your bad luck. He could also wield the cane, probably three or four stripes on each hand, or very often he would take the boys out into the porch to be caned.

I always thought Mr. and Mrs. Waldron were a fine example of a happy family, and they were very much respected. In the early days they kept a pony and tub as their means of transport.

Of course, the toilet facilities in those days were very primitive, they were flushed periodically from a small tank at the back of the building. In the early stages the water was pumped up from the Old Reading Room, that is the cottage on the other side of the road opposite the school. They then progressed somewhat and it came from a windmill up the fields on the Court Farm on the north side of the school. There was only one cold tap for the boys to wash their hands in a very small primitive three sided shed affair. There was also a small wash basin in the corner of the alcove up the other end of the large classroom with one cold tap mainly used by the girls. There was a door which opened out of this into the private backyard of the school house. The coal for the open classroom fires was kept in the cellar of the Reading Room cottage.

I will digress a little here to explain that the Reading Room was given to the parish as a recreation room by Mr. Arkwright of Hampton Court (I think he was what was termed in those days as Lord of the Manor), although it had been a dwelling house or small-holding prior to that.

Also I remember Mr. Walter Morgan Junior of Court Farm which adjoins the school premises, who used to take Sunday School, of which I was a member, and I must add he was extremely good in this office. Also he was a marvellous entertainer at all the concerts with a good singing voice to boot. The village was a very happy community in those days, everything seemed so tranquil no hurry and bustle and time did not seem so important.

A few people came from the outlying farms to Church and used to leave their ponies and traps round at the back of the Reading Room - this part had earlier been converted into stables.

Now I consider Mr. Waldron was quite brilliant in music for which he had attained his cap and gown. He always played the organ in church and, of course, used to accompany all the school concerts on the piano. I well remember one occasion another girl named Ethel Lloyd and I standing on a chair each singing 'Little Water Wagtail'. It was quite surprising the talent one could muster up around the village in those days. He also accompanied my mother singing solos in church. They had a very good choir, also the bells used to be rung regularly.

I think Mr. Waldron's favourite hobby was his bees. I remember a swarm invading my home and he very calmly came and dealt with them. One day a boy named Arthur Weaver very unfortunately had a bee enter his ear and he careered round the playground at a great pace. However Mr. Waldron's daughter, Rachel, saw him and came to the rescue with one of the old fashioned hat pins of that day and with some difficulty managed to extricate the bee!

Arthur Hodges, who was very polite and willing, was always chosen by Mr. Waldron to do his little odd jobs.

Mrs. Waldron used to give a ten minute session every morning for all the infants to tell her their little tales like small infants do - must tell teacher this and that. I even remember in that small break one or other of us dashing out to get the duster to give her shoes a little polish as both she and Mr. Waldron were always very smart and well turned out. After that small break it was apply yourself to lessons as the only playthings in the cupboard that I recall were some beads in small boxes. We regularly went out weather permitting, for what was known as drill. Mrs. Waldron used to have us line up and the first thing she ordered was handkerchiefs out and my word, it was woe betide those who failed to produce one. She said 'I do not mind if it is only clean tissue paper'. She then counted one, two, three, blow, after which she took us through the whole procedure of deep breathing, a speciality. Looking back I have often smiled for if a child happened to be absent and not well Mrs. Waldron would ask where the child was and you would invariably hear a voice pipe up 'Please teacher he is ill'. Mrs. Waldron would always ask -'Is he eating and drinking well and sleeping well at night?' the answer would come back 'Yes teacher'. Mrs. Waldron would then say 'There is no reason whatsoever why he should not attend school'.

Mrs. Waldron was always very meticulous in prompting any child to pronounce the correct christian name when referring to another child. She would not tolerate nicknames, if this ever happened she would look non-plussed and claim no knowledge of knowing them.

Mr. Waldron also took us through a very thorough procedure of drill, you really had to jump with arms upward stretch and knees full bend, etc. He also expected us to line up in the morning out in the playground before we marched into lessons. He used to patrol up and down the lines making sure they were very straight and orderly. He always inspected our footwear, again it was woe betide those who had failed to get a good shine on their shoes or failed to wash behind their ears. We were always expected to line up orderly and file into school in a very correct and quiet manner. In fact, in lesson time it was always expected that we kept as quiet as possible. You could often have heard a pin drop I am sure.

The children always brought their own sandwiches and naturally used to hang them in the porches. There was sometimes great consternation as the hound puppies which they kept at the adjoining Court Farm would come round and devour some of their lunch. Mr. Morgan Senior of Court Farm was one time master of the hounds so naturally he would have so many hounds from time to time to run on the farm.

They used to hold all the functions in those days in the school. They used to roll back the partition right the way down, and for dances the band used to assemble to play on the north side of the large classroom and the refreshments were spread along the side of the small classroom nearest to the church. There was much talk of building a Parish Hall. This of course they achieved in, I think, 1932. It entailed a great deal of voluntary work to raise the money but everyone banded together and they won through in the end. This was a great step forward for the village as they could then hold all the functions, meetings, etc., in the hall thus relieving the school of any disruption in the form of moving furniture and the like.

One must have some sympathy for Mr. Waldron and his family who after all were living in the same building.

The children did not leave school in those days until they reached the age of fourteen. Some of the boys were almost quite as tall as Mr. Waldron. I did mention earlier for the tendency to remain as quiet as possible in class, but I do remember how we used to chant the tables parrot fashion. Mrs. Waldron made thoroughly sure you knew right through to

your twelve times before you left her infant class. They used to keep a strict timetable
-always arithmetic first thing in the morning. Mr. Waldron maintained your brain was
clearer and the mind more receptive at this time. Mr. Waldron always took nature study in
the afternoons, he sometimes took us on a nature walk to gather a special flower or leaves
taking special notice we walked in an orderly file. On arrival back in school we often had
to draw this particular specimen and talk a thorough lesson concerning it. I do remember
a couple of times Mr. Waldron took us to find the one spot where the White Campion was
growing, he thought it was almost becoming extinct.

Geography lesson was always taken during an afternoon, we were expected to know
all the cotton towns, all the towns of the potteries and others. The same applied to
memorising all the dates in history, I well recall having to learn from 1800 - 1900.

I remember too how Mr. Waldron was a stickler for a child to show every part of the
working of a sum in arithmetic. I recall how on one or two occasions, a child had glimpsed
the answer to a certain sum in the answer book and, of course, written it down not realis-
ing Mr. Waldron had immediately seen through this ruse. Then, of course, followed the
folly of this foolish move. We often had to learn different poems and Mr. Waldron would
call upon a pupil haphazardly to go out in front of the class and recite a poem of your own
choice. I recited one called 'The Happy Workman's Song', it used to be a favourite of
mine and went like this:

> I live in a cottage and yonder it stands
> And while I can work with these two honest hands
> I'm as happy as they who have houses and lands
> Which nobody can deny
> I keep to my workmanship all the day long
> I sing and I whistle and this is my song
> Thank God that hath made me so lusty and strong
> Which nobody can deny.

Another girl named Maud Bayliss who lived at The Three Horse Shoes, Little
Cowarne, who was older than I, recited one about the rich man in his castle and the poor
man at his gate - unfortunately I just cannot memorise the title but it was very good and
she won it. If I remember rightly it was verified by the amount of applause of the
audience. I used to look up to Maud Bayliss, she was quite a nice looking girl. We girls
sometimes practised dancing round the back, we used to sing or hum a tune to get the
rhythm and it was Maud Bayliss who taught me my first dancing lessons there.

We always had a resident Rector in the village in those days. He regularly came to
school in the morning to give his religious address. As he entered the classroom door we
were all expected to immediately get to our feet with a 'Good Morning Sir'. At that particular time it was Bishop Iliff who used to visit us. He had been Bishop in China. He
quite frequently invited us Sunday School children to the rectory to tea. It was quite an
occasion too as his household really was run on oiled wheels. This was at the later new
built rectory just along the road from the school. He kept maids and an outside gardener
handy man. Both Bishop Iliff and his wife are buried in Pencombe churchyard.

Mr. Waldron also taught my father and I am sure my grandmother paid a small fee
per week when she attended.

Transport was unheard of in those days and some children had literally miles to walk to school in all weathers. Many I knew came across fields before coming into contact with the road. On dismissal from lessons in the afternoon you were not allowed to loiter around the school premises. It was at this time that Mr. and Mrs. Waldron invariably took their daily constitution, a good walk along the country lanes, and on one occasion it was at this time of day when two girls named Ida Lea and Ethel Bemand and I decided we would like an apple - well just down the road were two or three apple trees. I do not think they belonged to anyone. Two of us had already climbed the tree when along came Mr. Waldron. I literally jumped straight to the ground and, of course, we had some slaps around our legs and told to hurry off home.

Pencombe School photograph taken c1930 with Mr. Waldron and his grandson Gerald.

Back row l. to r. Margery Lane, Doris Jones, Daisy Baker, Betty Lewis, Mary Weaver, Ethel Lloyd, Edith Jones, ? , Ruth Legge, Molly Weaver

2nd row Phyllis Jones, Gwen Leighton, Ben Weaver, Phyllis Lloyd, ? , Annie Legge, ? , Joe Legge, Thomas Legge

Front row Ernest Dukes, Robert Bemand, Lewis Legge, Edward Legge, Arthur Dukes, Stanley Leighton, Eddy Jones, Leonard Jones

Thoughts On 'A Pencombe Ditty' and Miss Winifred Norbury

By A. IRENE SOUTHALL

Journal 3, 1980

There came a sailor from over sea,
To Bristol, long ago,
With a bag of gold, and his heart was free
He'd a handsome face to show.
He longed for a country life,
He looked for a pretty wife.

Chorus

If you want a wife for a country life
To Pencombe you must go.

He met a maid in a country lane;
Her voice was sweet and low,
Her cheek was touched with a vermeil stain,
Her brow was white as snow,
Her eyes were starry bright,
Her tresses spun of the Night.

Chorus

Quoth he - "I'll take you to Bristol town,
Where the great ships come and go,
And marry you there in a silken gown,"
The maiden whispered, No!
Tis I'll be a farmer's wife
And live a country life.

Chorus

"Then I'll live and die on the land I hold,
I'll learn to plough and sow,
I'll 'stank yon Pencombe Brook wi' gold,'
I've gold enough I trow."
The maiden blushed and said -
"I'm far too young to wed."

Chorus

The bells rang merrily down the dale,
The dainty brook did flow,
And there she stood in a silver veil
With bridesmaids all in a row.
The Arrow of Love was sped,
The pretty maid won and wed.

Chorus

Long life to all True men and brave,
All matrons that we know;
Long life to maidens gay or grave,
And the boy that bears the bow.
Let nought your souls affright!
Goodnight! Goodnight! Goodnight!

If you want a wife for a country life
To Pencombe you must go.

E.B.O.

Had you lived in Pencombe at the turn of the century you would have been familiar with the Ditty but now it is only a lingering memory.

The Ditty was written for the opening of the Billiard Room, Pencombe, on 29th February 1892 and dedicated to Miss Winifred Norbury, who sang it on that occasion. The Billiard Room was afterwards called the Reading Room and is now Townsend Cottage, opposite the School at Pencombe. The Rector, as was usual at the time, used to have students and the Arkwright family, the important local landowners and benefactors, gave the Billiard Room for the students and the villagers to provide entertainment. It also provided shelter for the horses and carriages of outlying farms when they attended church services and other functions.

A few years ago, what I like to think was one of the original song-sheets used at the opening of the Billiard Room was given to me. It had been printed by the Bromyard News on buff-coloured paper and was in a very fragile condition. On the back was a charming, tinted drawing of a winsome girl in a simple sailor dress, carrying a hat; the edge of her white and red striped petticoat and delicate pointed shoes were just visible. I was immediately captivated and felt I must find out all I could about her. Was she the local pin-up girl, I wondered, surely the verses in true Victorian style must have been written by a student and, deduced from the initials, the poet and the artist appeared to be of the same family. Perhaps Winifred was a member of the local Norbury family, but it later transpired she was not, and I felt rather downcast, but, like the Ancient Mariner, continued to tell my story to all who passed by and continued to question all likely individuals. Then Mrs. Edith Jones, who now lives at Townsend Cottage, told me she had sung it years ago and the tune was similar to that of the Lincolnshire Poacher but with slight variations and I was advised to get in touch with Mr. Arthur Jenkins, now living in Hereford, but a native of Pencombe, who still had strong local family ties and had been organist at Pencombe Church. He had been the accompanist when, on many convivial occasions, the Ditty had been sung, and eventually he played it for a group of our local W.I. members, who were practising before entertaining patients at Bromyard Hospital, when the husband of one of our members recorded it.

All this time Winifred Norbury was held in my imagination and, happily for me, the B.B.C. put on a television programme based on the characters of Elgar's Enigma Variations. Immediately I felt my Winifred must be W.N. and my saga continued. My husband and I visited Elgar's birthplace at Broadheath but the only relevant information we found was on posters giving details of appearances of Elgar and his friends, including Miss Winifred Norbury, at concerts in local villages. Then we went on a pilgrimage to get apples from Norbury's at Sherridge, near Malvern, and remembering that Elgar had at one time lived very near, we asked the lady at the pay-point if she knew if the family had any connection with the Winifred Norbury. Yes, she said, she was my husband's aunt, and she suggested I should contact her mother-in-law.

After several delays and frustrations I was able to get in touch with Mrs. Norbury senior. At first she thought I was just another enquirer about Elgar but when she knew it was Winifred in whom I was interested she was very kind and helpful. She told me that Winifred's father had had five daughters and then three sons, and she had married the youngest of the sons who was forty years of age when they were married and she was training to be a singer in Milan. Mrs. Norbury told me that Winifred had been of great help to Elgar in his early struggles and she must have had a very adventurous spirit in her day for she travelled all over the place with her concert party, even through Germany, and that was where she met Richter, the famous conductor, who conducted Elgar's 'Dream of Gerontius' in Dusseldorf where it was very well received, while the previous performance in London had been a flop. Richter later came to England and conducted it when everyone thought it was wonderful.

Of course nothing is proved, but I think I have found my Winifred Norbury who came to Pencombe and first sang 'A Pencombe Ditty'.

Bromyard Fire Services 1811-1978

By EDNA D. PEARSON

Journal 1, 1978

Perhaps the recent national strike by the firemen, although our Bromyard men did not join in the dispute, made us more conscious of the danger of fire.

Fire was always a calamity to be dreaded. Almost all mediaeval towns were attacked by the devastating element from time to time. Apart from conflagrations which threatened a whole town, fires which destroyed a part or even the whole of a single house were quite common. Since houses were frequently built of wood and plaster and sometimes had both thatched roofs and wooden chimneys, which afforded excellent fuel for the flames, it is hardly surprising that there were so many accidents.

Until the early 18th century Bromyard was largely a town of wood and plaster buildings. There is no record of such a disaster as happened, for example, to Tiverton in Devonshire when in 1598 the whole town was destroyed. Four devastating fires happened in Stratford-on-Avon in the 16th and 17th centuries and at Warwick in 1694 there was a fire which 'consumed a great part of the said town'. Sometimes after such a great disaster the Sovereign would grant a special brief empowering officers from the affected town to collect money from other towns and counties for the relief of the homeless and the rebuilding of the wasted streets. In 1694 Stratford-on-Avon sent £12 for the relief of the sufferers of the Warwick disaster. In the 18th century Bromyard churchwardens' accounts show several payments varying from 1/- to 5/- to compensate for loss. Most of these payments were from outside the Bromyard area. In 1759 the entry reads 'Gave one Faulk of Cradley Loss by ffire 5/-'. In 1760 'Gave Ann Jones and Son Loss by ffire from Brecknock 5/-'. In 1761, 'Gave a family from Sutton Loss by fire 2/6' and again 'Gave 2 men from two miles above Kington which lost all they had by fire 4/-'.

Fire fighting equipment was very simple and not very efficient, at first consisting of leather buckets, a ladder and a fire hook, or croom, which were stored in some public place. In Bromyard this would probably be beneath the old Market Hall in the Square until the building was demolished in 1846. The next stage was a rather cumbersome and heavy piece of equipment; a cistern mounted on wheels with a delivery pipe in the centre or at the end and a manually operated pump to force the water through. For some years this engine was stored in a recess at the back of the gallery which had been erected at the west end of the Parish Church in 1739.

The first efforts of organising a fire brigade were made by the London insurance companies. Each company had its own firemen who would only deal with those insured with that particular company. A wasteful and inefficient system which merged into the London Fire Engine Establishment in 1833 and in 1865 became the Metropolitan Fire Brigade. Insured premises were marked by a sign showing the name of the company offices. There were many of these signs, or fire marks, attached to buildings in Bromyard. In July 1886 Bromyard firemen were complaining that they had not been paid for their services at the disastrous fire in the High Street in March where several properties were involved. It was explained that the various insurance offices had to agree amongst themselves before the claims were met. The Clerk to the Parochial Committee was directed to write to the insurance offices to ascertain whether they were prepared to pay for the services of the Fire Brigade in case of their being called out to fires.

Some insurance companies must have maintained brigades in the county, for there is a record of the Norwich Union Insurance Brigade attending a fire at Lulsley in August 1899.

In the early years of the last century owners of large houses provided their own fire fighting equipment. There is a photograph of an engine manually propelled and worked, with the inscription 'Presented by R. Higginson to Mr. Barneby by Brockhampton, Herefordshire 1818'.

It must be remembered that for the machine to function the tank had first to be filled and if sufficient pressure of water was not available this had to be bucket-filled. It was probably a similar appliance that was presented to Bromyard in 1811 by Mrs. Buckley of Buckenhill. There is a photograph of a larger horse-drawn machine which was acquired by the town in 1870.

The perpetual shortage of water constantly frustrated the efforts of the volunteer firemen. There was no mains water supply until the beginning of this century. The town derived its water supply from 77 pumps of which 3 or 4 were public. In dry weather these pumps were often locked at night, and even sometimes during the day-time, to conserve the water.

The most disastrous fire of which we have records was in 1886 when an outbreak started at Imms, a cabinet maker, in High Street. Both engines were called out (the little engine of 1811 was still functioning) but water supply was poor. The fire, discovered at 2 a.m. was spreading rapidly. The police sent for assistance but Bromyard was only connected by telegraph to Leominster which could not be contacted. Finally the stationmaster sent a message to Shrub Hill, Worcester. Later messages were sent to Saltmarshe and Leominster. The Saltmarshe engine arrived at 4.30 a.m. but did not function properly. The Leominster Brigade arrived at 7 a.m. and the Worcester Brigade at 7.30 a.m. by which time the fire had destroyed two houses and completely gutted four adjoining premises. Mr. Imms lost his life, but his brother managed to escape. In the same year there was another serious fire at the Tannery in Pump Street. In spite of the usual shortage of water firemen managed to get control of the blaze but one of the adjoining cottages was pulled down to stop the fire spreading.

In the last century the volunteer firemen were often slow to turn out. The cry of 'Fire' was not always heard and the men had to be knocked up. In 1888 it was suggested that a firebell should be erected in the town. Later a fog horn worked by the police was purchased. After the second world war the air raid siren at the New Road Station was used and house bells were installed in firemen's homes; now each man is summoned through an individual 'bleep' system.

Before motor transport, horses were required to pull the heavy appliance outside the town. Frequently they could not be found and the Brigade could not answer the call or the

Bromyard Auxiliary Fire Brigade outside Nunwell House.

delay was so great that the building might be gutted before the firemen's arrival. There is an apparently congratulatory mention in the *Bromyard News* of 1884 of a fire at New Hampton: 'Although over 6 miles from Leominster in less than 1 hour 15 minutes the Leominster Fire Brigade was in action'.

In 1913 there was a fire at the Raven's Nest and when no horses could be found the firemen took up the shafts and the rest of the men pushed the engine up the Rhea where they were met with a horse. A similar effort was made as late as 1933 when the engine was pushed to a rick fire in Avenbury. Unfortunately, on arrival at the scene of the fire, the engine refused to function and the weary men watched the fire burn itself out.

With the increasing use of motor transport after the First World War, motor cars and vans were sometimes used to tow the old machine, which was not built to stand the extra speed of travel. Mr. Wilson, the coal merchant, offered the use of his lorry, often loaded ready for delivery. There was no time to unload and the coal travelled with the Brigade!

By 1910 the Urban District Council had taken over the control of the Brigade from the Parochial Committee and were endeavouring to organise the service on more efficient lines, but with no long-lasting success, and by 1930 the town was having to seek assistance from neighbouring Brigades. The transformation of the Bromyard Fire Brigade was largely due to the energy of Mr. U. J. G. Dancer, the Bromyard dental surgeon, and the incidence of the Second World War. Mr. Dancer, Chairman of the Fire Brigade Committee, was anxious to see a really efficient service. New equipment was provided, including helmets and tunics to distinguish the firemen from the public. In February 1936 a new G.P.M. Trailer pump was purchased at a cost of £390.14s.6d. In 1937 Parliament passed the Air Raid Precautions Act which required schemes to be prepared to include an emergency Fire Brigade Service and the recruiting of auxiliary firemen. Mr. Dancer prepared such a scheme which was accepted by the Government and a grant was received towards the costs.

By 1939 the Auxiliary Fire Brigade was fully equipped and very efficient and the Home Office was so pleased with progress that they made a further allotment of one large trailer pump. In 1941 all Brigades were taken over by the Government and could be ordered to man stations whose firemen were already called to the scene of enemy action or to go direct to the bombed areas. Bromyard Brigade distinguished themselves on several occasions in the blitzed areas and in 1942, except for Hereford, were said to be the best in the County.

An Act of Parliament in 1947 made County Councils and local Boroughs the Fire Authorities from April 1948.

Apart from outbreaks of fire the present very efficient Brigade of retained firemen is fully equipped to deal with other emergencies with which firemen have to contend. Water has been carried where local supply has failed, motor accidents have been dealt with, cows have been removed from ponds and a dog was rescued from the roof of the King's Arms! In the hot summer of 1976 the men were exhausted by the constant calls to deal with grass and hedge fires.

Various buildings have housed the engines through the years; first in Rowberry Street and then in Frog Lane, then to the premises behind the Falcon in Pump Street. In 1941 the U.D.C. bought from Newbolds, premises in the New Road which were used until they threatened to collapse and it was decided to build a modern station on the same site. The building, equipped with the most modern appliances, was opened with much ceremony in 1961 at a cost of £7,500.

Bromyard may feel justly proud of its efficient fire service which gives the town and the outlying districts a sense of security.

Report on Fire at Pencombe Court.

July 25th 1941.

A call by telephone was received at about 15.40 hrs. to attend a rick fire at the above Farm.

A crew with the Pulsometer pump was dispatched & found a rick burning, which was reported to have been set on fire by a small boy (evacuee) who had been playing with matches.

Water was obtained by damming the brook nearby and after some hours of hard work "damping down" & cutting out "the burning hay the fire was extinguished. More than three quarters of the rick was saved and the crew returned to the Station by 20 hrs.

Some very good work was done by the crew of five.

W.J. Frances
Chief Officer

Romano-British Grave at The Wells

Deerfold House,
Lingen,
Bucknell,
Salop.

11.11.71.

Dear Mrs. Waller,

The name brings back so many memories 'Wallers of Keep Hill', how few of the old names are still writing from the same old addresses. It does my heart good!

I am wondering how you got my name and address. Bertha Coape Arnold perhaps?

I must still have been in the schoolroom when the 'Roman?' remains were found at The Wells. I think that would be pre-1914 if I am correct and in those days very little was known and very little interest taken in archaeology, but I remember that Mother took some of the pottery to Mr. St. John, rector of Pencombe who had a nephew at the British Museum who reported that it was of 'Roman period not necessarily Roman'. I remember some was black, of a coarse grain and I think painted with some sort of rough glaze and had a moulded edge, the rest was red. The black was moulded with a rim, but all was broken. There were also some small pieces of burnt (calcined?) bone, and the whole collection was surrounded by 3 or 4 slabsy stones.

I don't think I have any of the pottery. We gave some to the Hereford Museum, they might be able from the curve of the black pottery to guess the size and shape of the vessel.

It was found in a most unlikely place, under 3 or 4 ft. of solid clay on the side of a bank, no sort of mound or barrow or even on the top of a hill but beside a ditch, the overflow from the top farmyard pond which ran through the garden to the two lower ponds, and Mother was making a large rock garden with large scree and rocky bluff and pools and a water garden. I expect all this has been ploughed out by now as no one can go in for such grandiose landscape gardening.

I always imagine that the whole thing was intact, a burial urn containing bones and possibly food vessels, but was smashed by the beefy varlets who were digging out the clay to make the rockery. So little interest was taken in those days that no further excavations were attempted and the whole thing planted up. We never found any flints, but then no one was sufficiently interested to search. One interesting point, the site was about 6 yards away from the mouth of a deep unfailing very cold spring.

I am sorry I have written this so hurriedly but it is very late. Do let me know if you can find out anything more.

Yours sincerely,

Molly King-King.

Roman Pottery at Grendon Bishop

By DAVID JONES

Journal 1, 1978

On 22nd January this year, the archaeological research group of the Woolhope Club visited Batchley, Grendon Bishop, to inspect the site where a quantity of pottery shards have been picked up in a field about a quarter of a mile east of the farm buildings.

There is a concentrated scatter of shards towards the top end of the field and the group found several pieces which Mrs Jean O'Donnell took away for closer examination. She has since been in touch to say that some of the pottery is Romano-British and other pieces date from the medieval period.

Several fragments of flint have also been found on the site and a crop mark has been seen at times which crosses the field in a straight line.

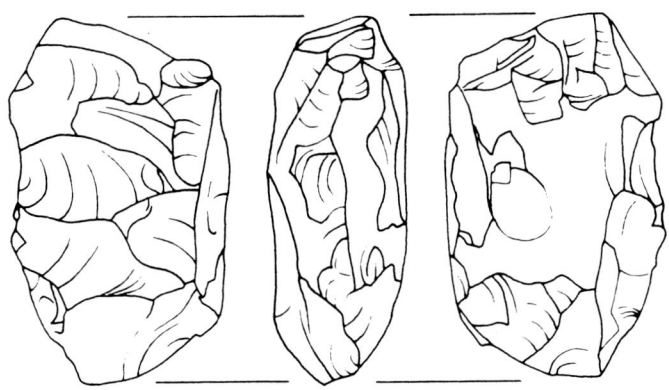

Neolithic axe-head(⅔).

A flint axe-head has been found at Batchley by Mary Wakefield-Jones. In the *Transactions of the Woolhope Naturalists Field Club* for 1988, J. D. Hurst wrote:

'It was a polished example of Neolithic date, and a notable feature was that it exhibited extensive signs of re-working subsequent to breakage. This demonstrates that, where flint was scarce, broken implements could be useful for producing smaller flake artefacts. When finally discarded the axe-head resembled a core, though with enough of the original polished surface surviving to indicate its primary function.'

Wolferlow

By DAPHNE DAVIES

Newsletter 9, 1976

This small parish lies discreetly at the north-eastern perimeter of the Hundred and abuts the shire boundary. Shaped rather like a sock or wellington boot its toe reaches into Collington, the heel is at High Lane on the Stourport road adjacent to Tedstone Wafre, and the leg is surrounded by Stoke Bliss, Hanley Childe and Upper Sapey. Its 1,500 acres are mostly on high ground up to 700′ above sea level.

We hope to visit this interesting parish in April when we meet at St. Andrew's Church. Earthworks are recorded in the vicinity of the church and can be clearly seen. In an adjacent field is probably the site of a deserted medieval village and in one corner is the village pound, with the Butts Field opposite. Wolferlow Court is a fine half-timbered house extended in the 17th century and the settlement appears to extend from the Court to Upper House across fields called Palmers Close, the Batches and Goose Green. Upper House has different stages of building spanning several hundred years; one especially fine feature is a six-panelled door with a decorative frieze at the top stated to be 17th century. One field name is a puzzle, it is Piece and Griffin; a theory put forward is that is may have belonged to a man called Rhys ap Griffith! Has anyone any other ideas?

Wolferlow from the north with crop marks indicating the deserted medieval village. (Cambridge University Collection: copyright reserved)

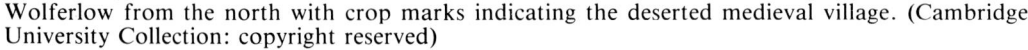

From Upper House towards Collington, down a steep drop along the old parish road now barely visible, lie the Underleys. Underley House was built of red brick in the early 19th century by a Bristol man of means called Where. The estate road runs north past the site of Middle Underley to Upper Underley and its large pond through which runs the parish boundary. This house is recorded by the Royal Commission on Historic Monuments as dating from medieval times. It was probably a single storey hall divided in the 16th century when the kitchen wing was added. It was largely rebuilt in the 18th century.

Climbing the ridge by the road passing Stoke Bliss Church one may reach Wolferlow Park. This former deer park of almost 100 acres was surrounded by a stone wall. Duncumb records deer belonging to Sir Edward Winnington being in the park at the beginning of the 19th century. The Park Farm built of brick shows at least two stages of building. William and Susanna Cooper's family lived here at least from 1840 until 1870 and at one time he had eleven children at home. Churchwarden at St. Andrew's in 1851, he would have travelled by the old roads past Poswick to reach the church. Now woodland divides the two farms. Poswick derives its name from Possa's Wick, an Anglo-Saxon dairy farm. The present house built in the last century stands adjacent to a much older site which has signs of early settlement. To the west of Poswick is Cockshut Coppice. Dr. Gelling has explained that cockshut was a means of catching woodcock with a net and beaters.

Nearby is the Heath Farm, a fine stone built farmhouse and buildings apparently all of one build perhaps at the turn of the 18th century. Much detail and care of thought is obvious in the style of the sills and lintels, the arches of the cart sheds and the large stone drinking trough. A most unusual feature is two ricks on stools and each stool topped by an iron cap. Samuel Drew lived here in 1840, but he also farmed Forty Acres. In 1851, aged 73, he was living at Forty Acres, near the Vicarage beyond the church, with his six-year-old grandson.

The Vicarage was built in the mid-19th century possibly when the church was largely rebuilt. Kempson, the architect, retained two Norman doorways and the chancel arch, and many of the old memorial tablets still adorn the walls. Beneath the tower the huge timbers are exposed and near the altar in stone effigy lies a lady in a wimple. Her gown falls in graceful pleats to her slippers which rest on a small dog. Her style of dress is said by Pevsner to be 'still in the 12th century and earlier 13th century tradition'. At this time the manor was held by the prioress and convent of Aconbury. One prioress, Joan of Ledbury, during the reign of Richard II, granted a lease to Walter Cruyk of Wolferlow. Later the manor was held by the Packingtons who sold to the Salweys in 1591. The Winningtons inherited through a Salwey heiress and the Winnington-Ingrams were connected with the parish into this century.

There are a few cottages in the parish. A settlement along High Lane seems to be built upon the roadside wastes and was no doubt maintained because of its proximity to the school, shop, inn and chapel, serving Upper Sapey and Tedstone Wafre. In 1851 there were eight cottages in this group including one in which lived Thomas Dallow, a carpenter employing two men and a wagoner.

This account of the parish of Wolferlow is merely a little dip into the past, a taste of its history. Detailed study continues especially regarding the people who lived on the land given its name by the Mercian Royal family, the family of King Offa - Wolfhaeda's low.

The Grants of Wolferlow

By MARGARET LANE

Journal 2, 1979

The recent publication of a biography of Frances Ridly Havergal, by Janet Grierson, brought back to me memories of Sunday afternoons long ago.

Frances Ridly Havergal was born in Worcestershire and her father became a canon of Worcester Cathedral. She was well known in the 19th century as the author of many hymns, some of which are in common use today, such as 'Take my life', 'Who is on the Lord's side?' and 'Saviour, Precious Saviour'. Also she wrote many religious books.

Her brother, Henry East Havergal, was the father of Cecilia Havergal who in 1883 married the Rev. Frederick Bickerton Grant, the future vicar of Wolferlow where he was the incumbent for forty-five years. Mrs. Grant was very proud of her famous aunt, whose talents she inherited being herself a composer and poet and a very cultured woman who studied French in Paris.

When I was a girl, a friend named Emma and I used to cycle to Wolferlow Church for 3 o'clock Evensong. We particularly enjoyed the musical part of the service. We received a kind welcome from the Vicar and Mrs. Grant, and their daughter Frances. Sometimes we were the only members of the congregation. Mrs. Grant was the organist, and her chants and anthems were sung in the services. She presided, shall we say, at the American organ, dressed very elegantly in rather old-style dresses, and wore a toque trimmed with flowers, with a veil, and sometimes with white feathers which quivered as she played.

Her daughter, Frances, led the singing, and came forward to the chancel step to sing her mother's anthems, and sometimes arias by Handel and Mendelssohn. She was a talented singer with a lovely contralto voice, and we were sure that with training she could have become a concert singer. The Harvest Festival was a great occasion with special music composed by Mrs. Grant with Frances coming forward to sing the Harvest anthem. After the service Frances would come to us, her long dress rustling, and give us tracts or copies of the anthems saying, 'Mama has sent you these.'

Mrs. Grant died in 1929 and the Vicar in 1934. Their daughter stayed on alone in the Vicarage, becoming rather a recluse, and died in 1955.

Tipton Hall -
opposite

Tipton Hall

Tedstone Delamere

By J. W. TONKIN

Journal 10, 1987

This is an interesting example of a medieval house which was largely rebuilt during the 17th century and added to again in the 18th and 19th.

There is little of the medieval house left today but there is sufficient evidence to show that there was such a building and to give some idea of its size. In the attic over the central block are two posts about 6 feet from the east wall. They are in the position of spere posts marking the line of the screen between the entry passage and the hall. If these are spere posts it means that the present east (kitchen) wing is probably still fulfilling its original function of a service wing to the hall.

The other cross-wing (parlour wing) seems to be later. It probably replaced an earlier wing, but it is possible that there was not a wing at this end in the original building. Thus it seems likely that there was a medieval house with a hall about 20 feet by 15 feet with a service cross-wing with kitchen and pantry downstairs and two chambers up and possibly a parlour wing at the other end. A glance at the back of the house shows the big, square panels in the service wing and the smaller, later panels in the parlour wing.

The original hall probably had an open hearth somewhere in the middle and the smoke got out through a louvre in the roof. Unfortunately, this original roof, which was probably well carved, has been entirely replaced by one of the 17th century.

This timber-framed, medieval house was much altered in the 17th century. It seems likely that this was done at two different periods. The parlour wing with its quite small, regular panelling looks as though it was built early in the century. It is quite big and originally contained two rooms on each of three floors and also a cellar running its full length. A stairway ran from top to bottom above and included the present cellar stairs; part of this is still in use but it has been extended. It seems that this wing may have replaced an earlier one but if so the latter was taken down completely, for the carpenters' marks on the hall side of the framing are of a 17th-century type and are a remarkably complete and intricate set. The beams in this wing have simple, run-off stops entirely different from those in the hall block. The bigger, front room would no doubt have been known as the great parlour and the smaller room behind as the little parlour.

It is probable that the big fireplace in the hall and the great stack that now hides most of the back wall of the hall block were built at this time, but it seems that the hall remained open to the roof for another fifty years or so. Also the through passage from front door to an opposite back door remained.

Later in the century, during the reign of Charles II, the hall was ceiled to make a first-floor and attics and probably it was re-roofed at the same time. The distinctive feature is the highly ornate type of stop at the ends of the beams. It is unusual and seems to date from about 1680.

This seems to have been the house described in an inventory of 1731. The rooms then were: Hall, Hall Chamber, a little room over the hall, Parlour, Room over the Parlour, maid's chamber, topploft, Servant men's room, cheese chamber, kitchen and back kitchen. The little room over the hall was probably over the entry passage, the maid's chamber may well have been the parlour attic, the topploft was probably the hall-block attic and the men's room and cheese chambers were quite likely over the kitchen and back kitchen. The greater number of rooms today is the result of later sub-divisions.

In the 18th century there were two more additions, the stairway extension between the hall stack and the parlour wing and the little room between this stack and the kitchen wing. The latter was built outside the old back doorway using this as an entrance, and has a corner fireplace typical of the time with a contemporary lintel. The stairway may have been added earlier in the century, perhaps even before the 1731 inventory. Its thinner timber-framing shows up clearly at the back of the house.

In the 19th century a brick china pantry was built on to the parlour with a room above it.

Thus the house while keeping its shape and size almost unaltered has been adapted for changing conditions and uses over a period of perhaps almost five hundred years and is a good example of the way houses have been changed in this way.

The big brick barn with its remains of hop kilns and cider press is an interesting building. I do not think it is the killhouse or the cider mill mentioned in the inventory. It is most likely an 18th-century building but later than 1731. It has big king-post trusses typical of that period as is also the brick work in English Garden Wall Bond. The inserted wall in the old hop end of the building is in a different bond, Flemish Stretcher, and added later, probably in the 19th century.

© 1972

Thomas Lane in his will mentions 'all that my capitall messuage or tenement wherein I do nowe inhabite called or known by the name of Tipton alias Tupton' and leaves it to his eldest son Benjamin.

Inventory of Thomas Lane of Tedstone Delamere, gent., dated 28 July 1731.

Wearing apparell and money in purse	£10 00 00
In the Parlour	
Goods	13 00 00
In the Room over the Parlour	
2 bedds and all appurtenances to them belonging	
and the other ffurniture in the same room	10 00 00
In the Hall chamber	
3 bedds and appurtenances and the rest of the	
ffurniture in the same room	5 00 00

In the cheese chamber	
Cheese	1 00 00
In a little room over the Hall	
1 bedd and bedsteads	2 00 00
In the Maids Chamber	
1 bedd	1 00 00
In the topploft	
A small parcell of ffeathers 1 grate and some lumber	10 00
In the Servant Mens room	
2 bedds and a tood of old hops	2 00 00
In the Hall	
1 clock and other goods	3 00 00
In the Kitchen	
Brass and pewter of all sorts and all other	
ffurniture there	7 00 00
In the Back Kitchen	
2 ffurnaces and other lumber	2 10 00
In the Killhouse	
2 killhares 1 malltmill 2 grates and other things	2 00 00
1 wagon 3 tumbrills 2 drays and 3 pair of harrows	10 00 00
Implements of husbandry of all sorts and tack of teem	4 00 00
Cidermill screws and hares and all appurtenances thereto	3 10 00
Hogsheads tubbs sceels coopers ware together with the	
cider and malt drink in them	13 00 00
In the Dayryhouse	
Utensils	1 00 00
3 yoke of oxen	30 00 00
9 cows and 1 bull	30 00 00
8 young beasts 6 yearling calves	20 00 00
3 horses and 1 colt	12 00 00
13 piggs 15 sheep	10 00 00
Thrashed corn in the house and the corn growing	
upon ground	20 00 00
** Lent grain growing upon the ground	15 00 00
Linnen of all sorts	1 00 00
Timber and cordwood fill upon the ground	2 00 00
Lumber and things omitted and fforgotten	10 00
	£231 00 00

Probate granted at Hereford 18 July 1732 to his son Benjamin Lane.

** Lent grain = spring wheat

Rural Rides

By MARTIN J. PERRY

Newsletter 7, 1974

The City of Hereford, and the five market towns within the county, have grown and remained as centres for local commerce, light industry, trading, markets and entertainment. However, without an efficient, regular and cheap means of transport for both goods and passengers to the outlying villages and farms, the growth of the market towns and even the city itself would have been slow and uncertain, as the pace of Herefordshire life quickened during the latter years of the last century. This is the basis of my research into the history of Herefordshire motor bus services.

The railways, so rapidly expanded and exploited during the 'mania' of the mid-19th century, made mass travel and nationwide communication cheap and easy, but their effect on the thinly populated, rural areas of Herefordshire was never great. Certainly, eager speculators, confident of a profitable return on their investments, sank thousands of pounds into the winding branch lines that spread across the map of the county during the 1860s and 1870s; the Golden Valley line; the Hay Railway; the Leominster & Kington; and, of course, the Worcester, Bromyard and Leominster. But the profits and the wealth never came; all were destined for hard lives and some an early demise - the Golden Valley line was to close to passenger traffic in the early 1930s, whilst the rest hung on into nationalisation and an ignominious death. Their days had been numbered from the outset, and one of the prime reasons for this was their inherent lack of flexibility; they were quite literally set in their ways, and as profits fell, costs rose, until the 'withdrawal of passenger facilities' drove home the final nail in the coffin of the 'permanent way'.

The story of public transport in Herefordshire is not, however, confined to the railways, for the gap between town and country was being filled by a more personal, flexible network of services; those of the village carrier. Many were the remote villages and hamlets through which, heading for the markets of the nearest town on the appointed day, the carriers' cart would rattle along the roughly-made roads. Laden with market produce on the inward journey, and with 'boughten goods' on the return, and carrying a few regular passengers for a couple of pence; it was from this modest makeshift beginning that the rural bus was to emerge.

The development of the internal combustion engine, and its application to the motor car was to bring the most sweeping changes to society. But, in those early days of the 1900s, it was with humour and scepticism that it was viewed. However, with some local foresight and accuracy the *Bromyard News & Record,* during November of 1906, observed: '...another of Bromyard's inhabitants was conveyed by motor to Burghill last week, and that apparently motoring in time will be of great advantage to the public. One started from Bromyard on Thursday evening, to take a party to Worcester theatre shortly after 7 p.m., and was back in Bromyard soon after eleven - if this is the order of the day, the railway company will not want to run many late trains...' The following year, 1907, the editor gave a further thoughtful assessment of the way trends in transport were to be: 'Bromyard is certainly not in a very sporting frame of mind just now, for only two booked by train to Colwall races last Monday; however it must be borne in mind that many preferred the quicker and more enjoyable way of getting there - namely by motor', and more pointedly: '...situated as we are, fourteen miles from anywhere, the motor car service will prove of great benefit, for instance Tenbury especially, which by some trains takes you half a day to get there ...'

The First World War was, in many respects, the great turning-point of all modern history, and in the story of public transport the war left its mark; a mark in itself the turning-point of that story. The end of the war saw men returning from the battlefields with new-found skills and training, not least of which was the ability to drive and to maintain motor vehicles. Further, large numbers of war-surplus cars and lorries came flooding onto the open market at cheap prices, and so for many it was only natural that the prospect of setting up local carriers, motor lorry and bus services was full of possibility.

Although Herefordshire had had its first regular motor-bus service as far back as 1908, when Connelly's began a service from Barr's Court to Whitecross in September of that year, this was to meet a sudden end in 1912 when the only vehicle (a 24-h.p. Milnes-Daimler open-top, 30-seat double decker) was destroyed by fire. It was not then until 1919 that the motor-bus reappeared on the roads of the county, when Mr Bird of Wigmore began a service to Hereford, and so this year must be taken as the actual starting-point for the true 'country bus'.

(At this point it is of interest to recall the 1907 report from the Bromyard newspaper - the use of the phrase 'motor car service' and its implications, and a report of a further 'motor car service' to theatricals in Stoke Lacy during April of that year, suggest the possibility that Bromyard may be able to lay a claim to the earliest of all motor-bus operations in the county. There is however, to the author's knowledge, nothing further, as yet to substantiate this possibility).

Nineteen-twenty saw the idea of regular bus services really take hold; Messrs James Fryer of Hereford commenced a service from St. Weonards, whilst other villages began to offer a market-day bus. Many of the vehicles at the time were motor-lorries, used for general haulage during the week, but fitted with wooden benches on market day and becoming passenger-carriers. Indeed, two of the county's most well-known present-day fleets began in this way: in 1920 a Canon Pyon cider-maker, Mr Yeomans, began to use his Ford T lorry (CJ 4206) to carry passengers to Hereford, and soon found this a well worthwhile proposition, and soon the lorry was permanently converted to a 14-seater, joined by another purpose-built Thornycroft bus, and thus started off the foundation of today's smart, modern luxury fleet. Likewise, Mr Bengry of Kingsland began to use his Austin lorry to carry people to local football matches, then to Leominster or Hereford market, and he too found that carrying fare-paying passengers was a worthwhile occupation. A second-hand Fiat charabanc was acquired, and later a Reo chara, of American manufacture. This was painted blue, and was shortly followed by two more Reos, one painted gold and called 'The Golden Queen', and the other yellow, named 'Primrose' - and thus the present-day fleet of Primrose Motors gained its name.

This Y type 30-seater Daimler bus first belonged to Staples of Ridgeway Cross and later was taken over by H. F. Taylor of Acton Beauchamp Transport.

Bromyard was not far behind in this, for March 1920 saw the commencement of regular services into the town from Hereford, Worcester and Clifton, provided by that well-known supporter of matters modern and technological, Mr. A. E. Pettifer. Although the B.M.M.O. (Midland Red) company, as a result of fortuitous circumstances bringing their operations to Worcester, had started a tentative service from Worcester as far back as 1915, and had also commenced a Hereford route in 1920, Mr. Pettifer was undeterred by such rivalry. It must, at this point, be appreciated that since the Road Traffic Act of 1930, all bus services must be licensed by government appointed Traffic Commissioners to prevent wasteful or dangerous competition, but in the 'pioneering days' of the 1910s such legality did not exist, and motor-bus operation was very much a free-for-all. No doubt situations such as were found in Bromyard, with rival buses running along the same roads, gave rise to much local splits of loyalty, as the rival companies were opposed or supported, as each vied with the other to gain the most custom.

Pettifers and 'the Red' were not the only providers of services into Bromyard, for the Clifton road was used by the equally expeditious Mr. Burnham, resident in that village. In fact, many of the surrounding villages had motor-buses travelling in on Thursday to the market - Matthews from Whitbourne; Howe's from Bishops Frome; Staples from Acton Beauchamp; Hancocks from Bishops Frome; Fryers from Hereford via Newtown or

Jenkins of Much Cowarne to name a few. Of these, it is of interest to note that Mr. Oliver Howe, Mr. A. J. Hancocks and Mr. Henry Jenkins had all been carriers, with horse and waggon, but came over to the use of motor transport as times had progressed.

Mr. Pettifer's first known motor-bus was a Sunbeam 25-h.p., seating 20, with the registration number CJ 1208. He also acquired, in 1920, a 35-h.p. Lancia, AB 8224. The following year a Wolseley 50-h.p., seating 35, arrived, along with a smart Karrier 40-h.p., also seating 35. This latter is of interest as it later passed to Mr. Alexander Matthews of Whitbourne, who fitted it with a home-built double deck body.

It was about this time that one of the most famous of Bromyard's vehicles appeared on the scene, the Daimler charabanc 'Nuff Sed'. No further details are at present known, however, of this or a further Daimler owned by Pettifers about the same time.

The Lancia acquired in 1920 must have been reliable and popular, as 1924 saw Mr Pettifer buy two more, with a further two in 1925. Although they ceased to be used as buses by 1936, one at least escaped the scrapheap, as it was converted to a lorry and employed around Mr Pettifer's Little Frome Estates (HL 2262).

Nineteen thirty-two was notable for the arrival in the town of a far more comfortable coach - indeed, the first of Pettifers' vehicles to which the term 'coach' can really be accurately applied. This was DF 5186, an American Reo, fitted with 20-seat coachwork, and purchased from the well-known Black & White fleet from Cheltenham.

An interesting purchase was made in 1935, when EA 5181 arrived. This was a 35-seater coach of A.J.S. manufacture, which had originated in the West Bromwich fleet of Messrs. Hills. It is, however, the fact that this vehicle is still surviving today that is of note. After five years work for Pettifers, EA 5181 was sold to Mr Arthur Moore of Great Witley, who pressed it into service in and around that village during the war. But, when its active lifetime drew to a close, it was not broken up, for with the great demand for mobility and acute shortage of buses at the end of the war, Mr Moore realised the possibility of completely rebuilding and renovating old vehicles as new. Thus, fitted with a new engine, luxury coachwork and given the new registration number HWP 569, the old A.J.S. carried on in service for a further ten years! However, even its final withdrawal from passenger service was not to be the end! Mr Moore's son had a large yacht, which often needed to be moved about the country to various waterways, or storage for the winter. So the bodywork of the old coach was removed, and replaced by a transporter for the boat; and in its new nautical role, the old vehicle carried on for a further couple of years, before being finally pensioned off to an honourable, but quiet retirement in the corner of a Great Witley orchard, where she remains today.

This interesting survival of a Pettifers vehicle is made all the more surprising by the fact that another of Mr Pettifer's one-time fleet remains in existence. This is a 1938 Leyland Cheetah coach, sold to Mr Burnham at Clifton in 1946, and stored for many years at Clifton, until purchased by Mr Morris early last year, and now brought back to Bromyard for possible restoration! It is more than strange that, of the mere 22 vehicles that were owned by the Pettifers bus fleet, two should still survive into 1975 - nearly thirty years after the business ceased to trade.

Ledger Book, 1821-1823, of Mr. Delabere Walker, Surgeon and Physician of Bromyard

By PHILIP H. CROSSKEY

Newsletter 3, 1972

Mr. Edward Walker of Hilltop, Martley, has been kind enough to let me look at an account book of one of his relatives, Mr. Delabere Walker, who was a physician and surgeon in Bromyard in the late 18th and early 19th centuries. He was born in 1763, one of a large family and had many relations in the Bromyard area. I have no details of his early life and training, but there is a record that land on the one side of the lane leading to Little Froome was owned by Mr. Delabere Walker in 1797.

Bromyard Parish Register records that five children, born to Meliora and Delabere Walker, were baptized in Bromyard:- Anne Maria on 13th November, 1795; Meliora on 28th April, 1797; Delabere, a boy, on 30th July, 1798; Charlotte on 25th March, 1800, and Harriott on 18th May, 1804. Rather sadly one finds that Delabere Walker, an infant, was buried on 27th November 1798, and Meliora, an infant, on 10th November 1802, whilst Meliora, wife of Delabere Walker, was buried on 24th August, 1804.

The ledger book runs from 1821-1823 and consists of entries of patients' names and addresses, dates attended and the treatments given. There is no record of the diseases or diagnoses made by the physician.

The district he visited was extensive and was equal in size to that covered by the present medical practice in Bromyard. Mr. Walker must have travelled entirely on horseback over the tracks and bridlepaths he knew so well. On one day, 11th February, 1821, he rode to see Mrs. Pytts at Kyre House and then to Mr. Lewis of Bachelors Bridge in Suckley parish, a cross-country journey of about fourteen miles. On another day, 31st March, 1823, he travelled to Mr. Storie at Froome, to the home of one of his family at Burton Court and to Mr. Lawrence at the Hedghouse. The largest number of country visits recorded for one day was on 18th August, 1822, when he visited the Reverend Mr. Barnaby at Saltmarsh, Mr. Potter at Stoke Lacy, the Reverend Mr. Apperley at Stoke Lacy and a Mr. Griffiths, near to Stoke Lacy.

A list of some of his patients, out of a total of 137 accounts, gives some idea of the extent of his district:- Mrs Lipscomb, Seapy (Sapey); Mr. Davies of Woolverlow Park; Mrs. Pytts, Kyre House; Mr. Walker of Hatfield; Mr. Holder at Hegdon, Pencombe; Mr. Bayliss of Moorhouse, Cowarne; Mrs. Bullock of Ocle Court, Ocle Pychard; Mr. Vevers of Yarkhill; Mr. Starling near the Nupend, Cradley; Mr. Farmer of Lulsley; Mrs. Harris at Gaines, Whitbourne. It can be seen that he attended anyone within a radius of seven or eight miles of Bromyard in any direction. He also served as physician to some of the poor in the parishes of Avenbury, Hatfield, Leominster, Pencombe, Ullenswicke (Ullingswick), and was paid by the Guardians of the Poor - sometimes more promptly than by his richer patients.

The entries in his book give us some idea of the different sorts of people he cared for. For instance, Mrs. Pytts of Kyre House employed a large staff and at various times there are records of attendances to Mr. Baker, Mrs. Smith, Miss Irvine, a coachman, a footman, cook, coachman's child, Hayes, Mr. Taylor, Mr. Geoffreys, a gardener, a housemaid, a servant man, besides Mrs. Pytts herself; some of the names listed may have been guests staying in the house. The Reverend Mr. Apperley at Stoke Lacy also had a large household to fill the Rectory. Mr. Walker attended Mrs. Apperley, Miss L., Miss G., Miss A., Miss Al, a nurse, a servant, Evans, a butler, Evans' child, servant maid, footman and Bubb - whoever he or she may have been Bubb certainly needed a fair amount of laxatives.

Amongst the doctor's patients were many of the local clergymen, solicitors, farmers, innkeepers, Miss Mason at the Library, shopkeepers such as Mr. Bray the butcher and Mrs. Willcox the mercer, and such varied tradesmen as breeches-maker, hatter, hairdresser, joiner, sexton etc.

It is impossible to deduce what illnesses were prevalent just from the types of medicines and pills which were dispensed. Many of the remedies he employed are still listed in the 25th edition of *Martindale's Extra Pharmacopoeia* (Pharmaceutical Press, London, 1967):-

Pilulae Guiac:	a mild diuretic.
Pil. Hydrarg:	mercury for its purgative effect.
Pil. Colcynth:	purgative.
Pil. Galbani:	a gum resin formerly used as an expectorant and in the treatment of nervous disorders.
Pulv. Rhei:	powdered rhubarb used as an astringent bitter.
Magnesium Carbonat:	antacid for treating dyspepsia.
Tincture of Valerian:	used as a depressant of the central nervous system in hysterical cases.
Mistura Myrrh:	a carminative, expectorant and mild diuretic.
Castor Oil:	only too well known for its purgative action.
Fol. Digitalis:	better known as powdered foxglove leaf was used first in a scientific manner by Dr. William Withering in Shropshire and described by him in 1785 in *An Account of the Foxglove*. It was used empirically by many physicians as a treatment for dropsy and as a heart stimulant.

Mr. Delabere Walker carried out many vaccinations on children at a charge of 5/- to 7/6; leeches were applied quite frequently at a charge of about 2/6 and he did many phlebotomies (drawing blood from a vein) at a charge of 2/6. He entered against Mr. Palmer of the Bridge the sum of 2/6 for introducing a catheter, presumably to draw off the urine, when the flow had been obstructed. There are entries for gargles, febrifuges, draughts for coughs and for constipation, poultices, plasters, and dressings etc. Dental surgery was also in his province; there are several entries for extractions of teeth at 1/- a time and for scarifying the gums of children.

Frequent were the calls for accidents such as broken bones, cuts, burns and scalds. Mr. Walker was surgeon as well as physician and set many limbs, an exacting task without X-rays to confirm the position of the bones after a fracture. Some patients had daily dressings applied by the doctor to wounds and ulcers, as there were no trained nurses who could be relied on to carry on treatment. Mrs. Willcox, a mercer of Bromyard, must have had an ulcer of the leg as Mr. Walker dressed it daily for many weeks in the autumn of 1821 and again in the spring of 1822; the good lady was charged nothing for this assiduous attention.

There is some mention of maternity cases as, for instance, on 27th March, 1822, when he attended Mrs. Potter at Stoke Lacy and charged £2.2.0. '... was detained some time extracting the placenta'. Several daily visits followed with prescriptions for aperient powders, castor oil etc. These were standard treatments of the time but the severe purges must have severely sapped the strength of the newly-delivered woman.

All these medicaments used by Mr. Walker must have been made up in his own dispensary. Some were probably carried by him on his rounds, but many must have been collected from the surgery for the patients. The doctor was assisted by a Mr. James Acton whose neat, legible handwriting records the attendances, the daily prescriptions and the charges; his is the signature for the receipt of many of the bills, but it is not possible to tell what professional standing he had. Very likely he did some of the visiting and dispensing. There were no chemists with ready-made pills so that everything had to be weighed and compounded from the basic ingredients. Pills were dispensed in variable quantities from 2 to 36; simple draughts were dispensed; other entries are for 8 fluid ounces of mixtures, 4 fluid ounces of linctus, 1½ fluid ounces of liniment; powders, plasters, lotions, bandages etc., are all entered in the ledger and charged at fairly standard rates for both rich and poor.

Charges for attendances varied from 7/6 to 10/6 depending a little on the distance involved; if the visit was during the night the charge was £1.1.0. Attendance on the poor was charged to Winslow parish at 2/6, but for Knightwick parish at 7/6. There are few records of visits to patients living in Bromyard itself which makes one wonder how many people consulted Mr. Walker in his surgery.

It is difficult to estimate what his annual income was as many of the bills were never paid and some patients never charged. The bill to Mr. Colley at the Falcon was balanced by washing; Mr. Williams of Sheep Street had his bill of £7.10.0 discharged by hauling coal in a barrow; Mr. Bitterley's bill of £6.5.6. was '... settled by cheese'; Mr. Benbow of Three Mills had his bill of £5.11.6. balanced by work done at the Mill; Mr. Walker Peel of Bromyard settled his bill of £5.0.0. with articles for building. Some of the accounts were marked bad or no charge and crossed out. The better off patients subsidized the poorer.

From the visits and dispensing recorded in this one account book the rough annual total comes to:- £340.0.0. in 1821, £340.0.0. in 1822, and £330.0.0. for 1823. But it is impossible to reckon his total annual income from the information given.

Mr. Delabere Walker died in Birmingham in 1838 aged 75 years; there is a large tombstone in Bromyard churchyard but, unfortunately, the inscription is so badly weathered that only the name remains.

Who Was Polly Planket?

By JOAN LEESE

Newsletter 9, 1976

Recently among the odd bits of paper on which I scribble memoranda to myself, only completely to forget them, I found one bearing these words:

> Polly Planket,
> gravedigger,
> 1st half 19th century?

The combination of such a name ('Enter Polly Planket in her best dimity ...'), such an occupation ('... and bearing a spade with which she strikes the First Body-Snatcher ...') and such a time when the range of female occupations was so restricted is too intriguing to ignore. The possibilities are endless - a big angular woman clumping along the Schallenge in hobnailed boots, or a small tidy body with a number of sturdy little sons to do the work for her, or a headstrong girl too proud to be kept by the Parish ...? but can anyone offer some facts?

Bromyard Churchyard before the removal of the gravestones.

INDEX OF PERSONS AND PLACES

Back cover   Translation of part of a charter describing the bounds
of an estate at Acton Beauchamp granted by King
Edgar to Pershore Abbey in 972. This charter,
which was possibly original, was attached to the
Great Pershore charter of 1282. (W. de G. Birch,
Cartularium Saxonicum, 1893).

Old parish boundary-rhyme from Bredenbury.